PREACHING FROM THE MINOR PROPHETS

Preaching

—— *from the* ——

Minor Prophets

Texts and Sermon Suggestions

Elizabeth Achtemeier

WILLIAM B. EERDMANS PUBLISHING COMPANY
GRAND RAPIDS, MICHIGAN / CAMBRIDGE, U.K.

© 1998 Wm. B. Eerdmans Publishing Co.
255 Jefferson Ave. S.E., Grand Rapids, Michigan 49503 /
P.O. Box 163, Cambridge CB3 9PU U.K.

Printed in the United States of America

03 02 01 00 99 98   7 6 5 4 3 2 1

Library of Congress Cataloging-in-Publication Data

Achtemeier, Elizabeth Rice, 1926- .
Preaching from the Minor Prophets : texts and sermon suggestions /
Elizabeth Achtemeier.
p.   cm.
ISBN 0-8028-4370-0 (pbk. : alk. paper)
1. Bible. O.T. Minor Prophets — Homiletical use. 2. Bible.
O.T. Minor Prophets — Sermon — Outlines, syllabi, etc. I. Title.
BS1560.A594   1998
251 — dc21   97-38554
CIP

*For Terry
and all the faithful
in PPL*

Contents

PREACHING FROM THE BOOK OF JOEL

PREACHING FROM THE BOOK OF AMOS

PREACHING FROM THE BOOK OF OBADIAH

PREACHING FROM THE BOOK OF JONAH

PREACHING FROM THE BOOK OF MICAH

PREACHING FROM THE BOOK OF NAHUM

PREACHING FROM THE BOOK OF HABAKKUK

PREACHING FROM THE BOOK OF ZEPHANIAH

PREACHING FROM THE BOOK OF HAGGAI

PREACHING FROM THE BOOK OF ZECHARIAH

PREACHING FROM THE BOOK OF MALACHI

Introduction

The Purpose of This Book

In the past few years, it has been my privilege to write commentaries on the twelve books of the Minor Prophets. The first six, Hosea through Micah, were treated in my book *Minor Prophets I* (The New International Biblical Commentary [Peabody, Mass: Hendrickson Publishers, Inc., 1996]). I dealt with the last six, Nahum through Malachi, in *Nahum — Malachi* (Interpretation: A Bible Commentary for Teaching and Preaching [Atlanta: John Knox Press, 1986]). Both of those commentaries were intended for preachers, teachers, and laity, and they give a full exposition of the prophecies of these not-so-minor prophets.

Having been treated to the wealth of preaching material in The Twelve, however, I realized there was still more to say. Indeed, the riches of the Word of God to be found in the Minor Prophets' writings are almost inexhaustible.

Despite the treasures in such a rich lode, the church and the pulpit have long neglected the wealth found there. Out of the sixty-six chapters that make up the Minor Prophets, the three-year lectionary put out by the Consultation on Common Texts specifies that only twelve passages from the Minor Prophets be used as the text for the day. Most of the designated texts occur in Cycle C of the three-year lectionary. Two texts are listed from Hosea, Joel, and Micah. One text is to be used from each of Amos, Jonah, Habakkuk, Zephaniah, Haggai, and Malachi. None is listed from Obadiah, Nahum, and Zechariah.

If a Bible study uses one of these prophetic books, it is usually Hosea or Amos. As a result, few people in our congregations are even

1

aware that there is a book of prophecy called Nahum or Zechariah. They know nothing about the content of Joel, Haggai, and Malachi. And usually such lack of knowledge is seen as totally inconsequential.

Yet these twelve books are an important part of the church's canon, writings that make up a portion of our authority for all faith and practice. Through these books the voice of the living God continues to speak. And through these books the God and Father of our Lord Jesus Christ is revealed, as he has worked in that span of salvation history that runs from Genesis through Revelation — that span in which you and I still stand and from which we find the basis for all our living.

The prophecies of The Twelve cover almost three centuries in God's plan of salvation. They deal with a wide variety of issues in the life of the people of God that are still very pertinent to the life of the church. Thus, if a preacher follows the lectionary exclusively and omits the witness of these prophets, he or she is not presenting the Word of God in its fullness. Certainly the lectionary is helpful, especially for beginning preachers, but once a preacher has learned to preach from a text and not from his or her seminary class notes, then the lectionary should be followed very flexibly and should be expanded to include many more passages from these prophets.

Because many of the texts from the Minor Prophets are unknown to the modern church, a preacher is not bound to a past tradition. There are few standard treatments of these texts, few preformed opinions about them, few familiar ways of dealing with them. The preacher confronting these unknown books is simply left with the Holy Spirit, to wrestle with the biblical text.

This volume is my attempt to participate in such wrestling. It is not intended to replace the commentaries on the Minor Prophets. Rather, its aim is to *supplement* such commentaries, to suggest further what might be said from the books of The Twelve. It presupposes the commentaries, but goes on further to connect the biblical texts with the life of modern-day congregations.

The Arrangement of This Book

All twelve of the Minor Prophets are dealt with in this volume, and for each, a standard arrangement is followed.

First, there is a list of suggested commentaries that the preacher may want to add to his or her library and that can afford further information about the prophetic text, as well as further suggestions for preaching from that text.

Second, there is a section giving the historical context of the prophetic book being used. The prophets' words do not reflect eternal principles or spiritual truths divorced from actual history. Rather, they are spoken into specific times in the life of the historical peoples of Israel and Judah who lived in the ancient country of Palestine. God actually did break into real human history with his words and actions, just as he breaks into ours. His deeds cannot be divorced from that historical setting.

The historical context given in each instance is very brief, however, designed to equip the preacher with only the basic historical knowledge that she or he needs in writing a sermon. For further historical information, the preacher can consult the commentaries.

Third, for each prophetic book there is a section that treats the theological context of the passages under consideration. Nothing is more important in sermon preparation than knowing the context of any pericope, because very often the context determines in large measure the meaning of the single passages. One needs to know the whole shape of Hosea's thought, for example, before his message in one passage can be fully understood.

Once again, however, treatments of theological context are rather brief, furnishing the preacher with the basic outlines of the prophet's thought. For further exposition, the preacher is directed to the commentaries.

Finally, for each prophet, there are sections dealing with selected texts. For each text employed, three elements are provided. First, there is a brief treatment of "Features to Note in the Text." This is designed to point to emphases in the text, to meanings of particular words or phrases, and to rhetorical structures of the text. By studying such features, it is hoped that the preacher will become drawn into the text and thoroughly acquainted with its meaning and message. Only by "living into" the text, as it were, can the preacher truly preach its message.

Second, a suggested sermon title is given that it is hoped will arouse the interest of a congregation. Congregations often must be prompted to *want* to listen to a sermon, and very often a sermon title can arouse that eagerness. None of the sermon titles are binding on the preacher, of course. They are simply suggestions.

Third, under each suggested sermon title there follows a homiletical exposition given from the text. Some of these are brief, some are rather lengthy, but *no one of them is a complete sermon*, nor is any sermon outline furnished in this book. Rather, the homiletical sections are designed simply to stimulate the thought of the preacher about the text and to suggest *possible* sermonic uses of the text.

No preacher should rely solely on another person's sermon outline or homiletic exposition. Many preachers do so, employing books of sermon outlines from which to preach. Some even steal sermons from others: some of my published sermons have suffered this fate. But such "borrowing" indicates that the preacher has not personally studied and wrestled with the text for herself or himself and so has no possibility of preaching the Word of God that comes through the text. God has called each of us, with our distinctive gifts and personalities, to proclaim his Word. He wishes his Word to come through the medium of our person; and to simply borrow someone else's sermon is to fail God's purpose for us.

The Biblical Text Used

Unless otherwise specified, the biblical texts and quotations used in this volume are taken from the Revised Standard Version of the Bible. There are many — indeed, far too many — different translations available these days; one of the sources of disunity in the church is the fact that we are not now all reading one version of the Scriptures.

Assessing the variety of translations on the market, however, I have come to the conclusion that the most accurate — and beautiful — translation of the biblical text is still the RSV. While the NRSV has correctly used inclusive language for human beings, I, along with many scholars, have concluded that it considerably tones down the original force of the Hebrew and Greek and sometimes destroys biblical linguistic structures. Every translation of the Bible has its faults, of course; there is no substitute for the original languages. But I believe those faults to be fewer in the RSV than in other translations.

It is my hope, in writing this volume, that it will aid in the proclamation of the Word of God that has been handed down to us through the preaching and writing of God's prophets. Their witness is a gracious gift of life to us and our congregations. We are called, as stewards of these life-giving mysteries of God, to preserve their words uncorrupted and faithfully to hand them on.

Preaching from the Book of Hosea

Recommended Commentaries

Elizabeth Achtemeier. *Minor Prophets I.* New International Biblical
　　Commentary. Peabody, Mass: Hendrickson Publishers, 1996.
James Luther Mays. *Hosea.* The Old Testament Library. Philadelphia:
　　Westminster Press, 1969.
Hans Walter Wolff. *Hosea.* Hermeneia. Philadelphia: Fortress Press, En-
　　glish translation, 1974.

The Historical Context

The words that we find in the Book of Hosea were delivered by that
prophet sometime between 750 and 723 B.C. to the inhabitants of the
northern kingdom of Israel, shortly before the ten northern tribes in
that kingdom fell to the troops of the Assyrian Empire under the leadership of Sargon II (721-705 B.C.). Hosea does not mention the event, but
in 721 B.C., the population of northern Israel was deported and disappeared from history, their land being taken over by foreigners.

　　Hosea himself was undoubtedly a resident of the north. After his
country was captured, either he or his disciples fled to the southern
kingdom of Judah, where his book was assembled in its present order
and biographical material and a few Judean additions were made to it.

　　When Hosea began his ministry, his country was peaceful and
prosperous under the leadership of Jeroboam II (786-746 B.C.) of the
Jehu dynasty. There was, however, a great economic gap between the

well-to-do and the poor, often fostered by corrupt courts of law and a breakdown in public morality. In addition, religious practice and worship were everywhere syncretistically combined with the beliefs and practices of the cult of Baal, the Canaanite god of fertility.

When Jeroboam's son, Zechariah, was assassinated in 745 B.C. after only six months' rule, the monarchy was beset by total instability. Five different kings succeeded one another over a period of twelve years, four of them falling victim to political assassination, as Assyrian and anti-Assyrian factions within the court vied for political power. The final fall to Assyria occurred when the last king, Hoshea ben Elah (732-724 B.C.), attempted to free the country from the Assyrian yoke by appealing to Egypt for military aid.

The Theological Context

Most important when preaching from Hosea is the fact that Hosea speaks within the context of God's covenant with Israel. Within that covenant context, God's relation to Israel is that of Father and of Husband — in short, a relation of deepest devotion.

God created Israel when he delivered them from Egypt — their redemption made them a people. At the same time, God adopted Israel as his beloved son (Hos. 11:1; Exod. 4:22-23; Jer. 31:9, et al.).

More prominent in Hosea is the thought that God is the Husband of Israel, wooing her in the time of the wilderness wanderings (Hos. 2:14-15), marrying her (2:16; cf. 2:2), providing for her needs (cf. 2:8), and cherishing and loving her with all his heart (cf. 11:8). (Cf. Isa. 54:5-6; Jer. 31:32; cf. 3:1, 20).

Thus the covenant relationship in Hosea and, indeed, throughout much of the Old Testament is seen not as a legal contract fulfilled by obedience to the law, but a relationship of the deepest intimacy and love. God "knew" Israel in the wilderness (13:5), like a husband knows his beloved wife, and Israel is to know him in return with a love characterizing all that knowledge.

The question with which God therefore wrestles in Hosea is what to do with Israel when she does not meet his expectations for knowledge of him and covenant love and faithfulness toward him.

Such wrestling is manifested in two ways in the book. First, there are God's questions: "What shall I do with you, O Ephraim?" (6:4); "How can I give you up, O Ephraim? How can I hand you over, O Israel?" (11:8); "O Ephraim, what have I to do with idols?" (14:8). But second, God's struggle over his unfaithful and adulterous bride Israel is mirrored in Hosea's suffering over his harlotrous wife, Gomer.

The preacher ought not to conclude that Hosea arrives at his message by reflection on his life with Gomer. Just the opposite is true. Hosea receives his words that he must preach first of all through divine revelation that comes from without, from God. In the light of that revelation, he is then commanded to act out what God is going through with Israel — to be the flesh-and-blood portrayal of God's relationship with his unfaithful folk. Thus, chapters 1 to 3 in Hosea are, in large measure, an introductory encapsulation of what follows in chapters 4 through 14, illumining how Hosea's words are to be understood.

Hosea divorces Gomer, because God has nullified his covenant relationship with Israel: ". . . you are not my people and I am not your God" (1:9). Instead of clinging to her divine Husband, Israel has run after the baals, believing them to be the source of her prosperity and fertility in the land. Instead of relying on the strength and security given her by her Father and Husband, Israel has turned to foreign alliances and put her trust in military prowess for the protection of her life. She gives lip-service to her God (6:1-3), but she does not know and trust and love him.

Can such a sinful people amend their ways? Hosea's answer is "No." A "spirit of harlotry" (4:12; 5:4) has "wrapped them in its wings" (4:19), so they cannot escape it, and they have no possibility within themselves for amendment: "Their deeds do not permit them to return to their God. For the spirit of harlotry is within them, and they know not the Lord" (5:4). Hosea states the impossibility of escaping from what the apostle Paul would later call "slavery to sin." Israel is therefore doomed to that destruction which she subsequently suffers at the hands of God's medium, the Assyrian Empire (5:14; 13:7-8, 9).

Hosea is speaking before Israel finally falls to Assyria, however, and he therefore announces what must occur if Israel is to be saved from death. If Israel's ways are to change, only God can work the amendment, and if Israel is to be saved from destruction, only God can accomplish such deliverance. In short, God must do for Israel what she cannot do for herself.

The glad message of the book, then, is that God will indeed work his transformation of Israel's life and deliver her from the destruction that she deserves (11:9-11; 14:1-8). As symbol of that fact, the prophet takes back his harlotrous wife Gomer (3:1-4).

But the *manner* of Israel's deliverance is quite astounding. As in the much later prophecies of Second Isaiah, God will forget Israel's past (cf. Isa. 43:18-19) and begin his history with her all over again, sending her back to Egypt (cf. 8:13; 9:3), wooing her as a young lover in the wilderness (Hos. 2:14-15), and then betrothing her to himself with the betrothal gifts of righteousness, justice, covenant love, faithfulness, and knowledge (2:19-20). At the same time, he will remove the threat of unfaithfulness and death from her life, by removing her other lovers, the baals (cf. 2:6-7; 3:4), and by abolishing the natural and historical threats to her life (2:16-18). The result will be that Israel will return wholeheartedly to her God (as Gomer will return to Hosea, 3:3-5), to enjoy the fullness of life given to those who truly love and obey God (14:1-8).

The intriguing fact about the theology of Hosea is that its promised transformation and salvation of Israel's life do not take place during Hosea's lifetime or at any time within the history covered by the Old Testament. As with Second Isaiah, the promise remains entirely future.

The preacher therefore has to ask if Hosea's words were ever fulfilled. Was there ever a time when God began his history with his covenant people all over again? Has there ever been a time when the Lord has delivered his people from their slavery to sin and given them the power to return to him in faithfulness and steadfast love and knowledge?

The gospel according to Matthew announces that there has. Linking its good news always with that of the Old Testament, Matthew tells of the new beginning of God's work with his covenant people. Israel is set back once again in Egypt, as in Hosea 11:1, but this time, Israel the son, is Jesus Christ:

> And [Joseph] rose and took the child and his mother by night, and departed to Egypt, and remained there until the death of Herod. This was to fulfill what the Lord had spoken by the prophet, "Out of Egypt have I called my son." (Matt. 2:14-15)

So begins God's recapitulation of his saving history, as foretold by Hosea.

The story unfolds, then, through all the New Testament witnesses — this time the account of the Son who does not go away from his Father as Israel did (Hos. 11:2), but who is faithful even to death on the cross. And the announcement is made that those who participate in Jesus Christ through faith (1 Cor. 10:16) are given his new Spirit (Rom. 5:5; 8:9-11, etc.) whereby they are once again God's beloved children (Rom. 8:14-15), God's Israel in Christ (Gal. 6:16; cf. 1 Pet. 2:9-10) or, in the other figure, his bride (2 Cor. 11:2), who will finally be without spot or blemish (Eph. 5:27; 2 Pet. 3:14). Indeed, at the end, Israel of the Old Testament will be saved with the Israel of the New (Rom. 11:25-26), and God's history with his covenant people will be brought to its final goal.

Despite the fact that Hosea, like all the prophets, envisions a future that finally finds its fulfillment in Jesus Christ, the minister who preaches from Hosea should not begin with a text from the prophet and move immediately into the New Testament's proclamation of God's victory over Israel's sin. Hosea's message concerns not only the love of God but also the judgments of God, and it witnesses to the Lord's suffering because of those judgments. Those judgments are intended also for Christians, for we too are Israel, joined to the commonwealth of Israel (Eph. 2:11-13), grafted into her root (Rom. 11:17-24), and made partakers of her covenant through the death of Jesus Christ (Jer. 31:31-34; 1 Cor. 11:25). Israel's story is the story of our lives, writ large on the Old Testament's pages, and we need to hear the whole story before we are told that we may be saved.

What follows, therefore, is a selection of possible sermon texts from Hosea that may aid the preacher in proclaiming that entirety.

HOSEA 1:1-8

This passage forms a portion of the stated Old Testament reading for Pentecost 17C (or, as some call it, the 17th Sunday in Ordinary Time in Cycle C). However, the lectionary extends the passage through 1:11 and pairs it with Psalm 85; Colossians 2:6-15 (16-19); and Luke 11:1-13, thus turning its primary message into one of hope and salvation. It really forms a separate piece from 1:10–2:1 and should be interpreted by itself.

Features to Note in the Text

In v. 2, the Lord commands, "Go, take. . . ." The verbs in v. 3 are the same: "So he went and took. . . ."

The important word "for" occurs four times and furnishes the reason for what has been said previously: "*for* the land commits great harlotry . . ." (v. 2); "*for* yet a little while, and I will punish . . ." (v. 4); "*for* I will no more have pity . . ." (v. 6); "*for* you are not my people . . ." (v. 9).

Hosea performs in this passage what are known as prophetic symbolic actions. They are "signs" or symbols of God's present and future actions toward Israel. In fact, in biblical understanding, they inaugurate those actions.

Hosea is commanded to marry "a woman of harlotry," an *'eset zenunim*, v. 2. Gomer is not a faithful virgin when Hosea marries her. She is already a harlot, as Israel, God's bride, is already a harlot. Otherwise the marriage "sign" would have no meaning. This probably means that Gomer has given herself, either once or often, to prostitution in the cult of Baal, the Canaanite god of fertility. The pagan belief was that by the exercise of sexual intercourse in the worship of Baal, that god would be coerced, through sympathetic magic, to impregnate the mother goddess of the land and ensure its fertility.

Only one child is explicitly said to have been fathered by the prophet (v. 3; cf. vv. 6, 8). This child, Gomer's first, is symbolically named Jezreel, v. 5, because King Jehu of Judah, whose dynasty began at Jezreel, fostered the syncretistic worship of Baal (2 Kings 10:29-31). The verse predicts the military defeat of Israel and of the Jehu dynasty at the hands of the Assyrian ruler, Tiglath-pileser III, in 733 B.C.

Lô-ruḥâmâh, the second child, is named "Not pitied," v. 6. The verb "to pity" in the Hebrew *(râḥam)* means to have sympathy for the need and dependence of another. Thus, the Lord will no longer be moved by the need of his people, who are totally dependent on him for their life.

The third child, Lô-'amî, "Not my people," v. 8, is the sign of God's annulment of his covenant relationship with Israel. Throughout the Old Testament, the covenant formula states, "I will be your God, and you shall be my people" (Exod. 6:7; Levit. 26:12; Jer. 7:23; 11:4, et al.). Here the Lord declares that the Israelites are no longer his covenant people. He has divorced his bride Israel.

Sermon Possibilities

1. Immediate Obedience

There is no hesitation on Hosea's part to obey the awful command that God gives him, v. 2. Here we find none of Moses' stalling and excuses: "Who am I that I should go to Pharaoh . . . ?"; "They will not listen to me"; "I am slow of speech and of tongue." There is none of Jeremiah's pleading about his youthful lack of experience. There is not even Isaiah's agonized question about how long he must preach. No. God says, "Go, take," and Hosea "went and took," v. 3.

This is the same unquestioning obedience to God's Word that we read about in Genesis 22, when Abraham is commanded to sacrifice Isaac, the same immediate response that Peter and Andrew, James and John make when they leave their net and boats and servants and follow the Master (Mark 1:16-19 and parallels). There are no conditions attached to the agreement, no calculation of mitigating circumstances, no consideration given to personal feelings, as we find among others who are summoned (Luke 9:57-62). No. These faithful servants of God are summoned and they obey. And surely the same unquestioning obedience is demanded of all of us who call ourselves Christians.

But all sorts of questions immediately stop us in our tracks. How do we know that it is really God who has spoken to us? God speaks to us through the written and spoken Word, through Bible and sermon, but is the content of the Word absolutely clear? There seems to be considerable scholarly disagreement about what the Bible means, and the preacher has his own opinions. Maybe we should form a committee and study the issue, or assign a task force to write a denominational position paper. Let's not be too hasty in deciding what God wants us to do, especially if the Word of command contradicts the accepted standards of our society, as the Word to Hosea did.

By noting such doubts of modern churchgoers, the preacher has the opportunity with this Hosea passage to examine any one of a number of questions: What is the basis of Christian certainty about the will of God? How is the Bible illumined and made true for us by the Holy Spirit? What does 1 John 4:1 mean when it says "test the spirits"? How is the life of Christian discipleship different from that of the society around us? How do prayer and the fellowship of the church enter into our decisions? Can we know the will of God?

Then, knowing what God wants us to do, how can we do it? Are there no qualifying circumstances that have to be taken into consideration? How can we balance our responsibility to family, job, and society with our responsibility to God? Do we have the power within ourselves to do God's will? What are the assurances given us by God when we seek to obey his command? What will be the consequences if we do not obey?

Or finally, what is God seeking to do by giving us some particular command in his Word? What are his purpose and goal? Is our inclusion in his purpose the reason for our life?

The preacher is given the occasion, using this passage from Hosea, to examine the source, certainty, and life of Christian discipleship.

2. God's Shocking Command

There are many passages in the Scriptures that bother us and offend our sensibilities — such as God's command to sacrifice Isaac, or Elijah's slaughter of the 850 prophets of Baal and Asherah, or the Psalmists' hateful vengeance toward their enemies. We typically try to soften such passages by reinterpretation, or we ignore them altogether. Such has certainly been the fate of this command from God to Hosea. Many commentators have maintained that Gomer was innocent and pure when Hosea married her, and that she did not fall into harlotry until several years into the marriage.

Surely God would not command his prophet to marry a harlot — and a Baal worshiper at that! Faithful people are not to be mated with unbelievers (2 Cor. 6:14). Then, too, imagine what the neighbors would say about such a marriage! Hosea's father and mother certainly would not approve such a mismatch, and would Hosea be so callous as to ignore their parental concern? Would he go so far as to give them illegitimate grandchildren?

We take offense at some of the actions of God that are reported to us in the Scriptures. These days some persons even take offense at the cross — all that bloody suffering and "abuse" (it is said) of his Son by the Father! God is a God of compassion and love, of quiet peacefulness and understanding mercy, we believe, and we should not connect him with the violence and blood, the suffering and evil of human beings.

The point is that *we* have connected him with all those evils. God is a God of peace, to be sure (Rom. 15:33; 1 Cor. 14:33). But Israel is a harlot, and we are harlots, delving deeply into evil. And so our God of peace and mercy and infinite compassion has to deal with our bloodshed and violence, our hatreds and prides and angers, our rebellions and unfaithfulness to his will — all those symptoms of our deep-seated sin that bring so much suffering upon us. And precisely because he is a God of compassion and mercy, of forgiveness and love, he takes all of those evils upon himself and suffers them in our place, confronting them head-on upon a cross in order that we may be redeemed from them.

> What thou, my Lord, hast suffered
> Was all for sinners' gain.
> Mine, mine was the transgression,
> But thine the deadly pain.[1]

So it is that God suffers in the time of Hosea, as he suffers still today, and Hosea, given this awful command to marry a harlot, is the living sign of that divine suffering. If we try to soften the text, we miss its theological meaning.

The preacher has the opportunity with this text to speak of the character of this God who will not abandon us to our evil, who suffers because of it, and who realistically confronts and triumphs over it.

3. Will God Reject Us?

God annuls his covenant with Israel, according to this passage, the covenant that he made with her at Sinai (Exod. 24:1-11) and that was promised to Abraham as "everlasting" (Gen. 17:7), the covenant that our Lord renewed with the church at the Last Supper (1 Cor. 11:23-26). God divorces his bride. When Israel rejects her divine Husband, he rejects her.

God's actions here contradict everything that our careless society presupposes about God. In the opinion of many, God never rejects anyone. He is always a tenderly forgiving God, no matter what we do, accepting us as we are and overlooking every wrongdoing. Indeed, God delights in our company, and we do him a favor when we worship him. Some even think that God needs them and cannot do without them — a thought that Israel entertained in her prideful moments.

---

1. Second stanza, *O Sacred Head Now Wounded.* Ascribed to Bernard of Clairvaux.

For those of New Testament faith, this passage seems contrary to the promise of God, that nothing can separate us from the love of God in Christ Jesus our Lord (Rom. 8:38-39), although Paul does not mention the effect of our sin in that text. But we also have long held the doctrine of election, whereby "they whom God hath accepted in his Beloved, effectually called and sanctified by his Spirit, can neither totally nor finally fall away from the state of grace . . . ,"[2] although

> they may, through the temptations of Satan and of the world, the prevalence of corruption remaining in them, and the neglect of the means of their preservation, fall into grievous sins; and for a time continue therein: whereby they incur God's displeasure, and grieve his Holy Spirit; come to be deprived of some measure of their graces and comforts; have their hearts hardened, and their consciences wounded; hurt and scandalize others, and bring temporal judgments upon themselves.[3]

As we shall later see in Hosea, God does not finally reject his chosen people Israel. But certainly Hosea announces those "temporal judgments" upon Israel in the prophecies that follow in his book. Israel is here in Hosea 1:9 separated from her God, and this passage furnishes the preacher the opportunity to deal with the seriousness of sin in God's eyes, with the very real fact of God's judgment upon sin, and above all, with the consequences of being divorced from God. This latter leads directly into the final preaching possibility:

4. When God Is Absent

We live in a secular world, that is, a world in which we think God is absent. We do not believe that he sustains and controls the processes of nature: the cosmos, we assume, proceeds entirely by natural law. We do not believe that God is in charge of international relations: those are mostly determined by politicians and military and multinational corporations. And many do not believe that their personal lives are sustained and guided by God: what happens to a person is largely a matter of genes, of environment, of luck, and of personal ambition, intelligence,

2. *The Westminster Confession,* ch. 21, 1.
3. Ibid., ch. 19, 3.

planning, and energy. As T. S. Eliot says, "We invent ourselves." So God has no hand in much of anything, other than perhaps having created everything in the first place (and for some people, even that is problematical).

The announcement of Hosea, however, is that human life and all of its circumstances are dependent on God. God divorces his people Israel; because of her sin, she is without him in the world. And the prophet spells out the consequences of that divine absence in all of his preaching that follows.

Israel, in the time of Hosea, has looked to Baal for the source of her life. It is that Canaanite god of fertility, she thinks, that furnishes her all of her material necessities (cf. 2:8-13; 8:7), just as it is military might, she believes, that gives her security in the world of nations (cf. 6:13; 7:8-11; 8:8-10; 12:1).

But Hosea proclaims that material goods, security, and life itself come only from God (ch. 12), and that apart from the Lord, she is without fecundity (9:11), fading away and dying in old age (7:9) or never coming to birth (13:12-13), without help from any quarter or any human power (5:14; 13:4-8).

The preacher has the opening here to speak about our total dependence on God in every area of our lives.

HOSEA 2:14-23

Verses 14-20 in this passage form the stated lection for the eighth Sunday in Epiphany in Cycle B. The verses are appropriately paired with 2 Corinthians 3:1-6, which emphasize God's new covenant and the sufficiency that we have from God alone; with Mark 2:13-22, in which Jesus proclaims that he has come to call sinners and not the righteous; and with Psalm 103:1-13, 22, in which God's merciful forgiveness is celebrated. All of these thoughts are presupposed in the Hosea text.

Features to Note in the Text

God speaks in the passage, and the actions that are promised are God's alone. The emphasis is on his "I": "I will allure" (v. 14); "I will give"

(v. 15); "I will remove" (v. 17); "I will make" (v. 18); "I will abolish" (v. 18); "I will betroth" (vv. 19, 20), etc. Israel cannot save herself.

There is a twofold use of "in that day" (vv. 16, 21), which signifies an indeterminate time in the future when God brings his purpose to fulfillment in a new age.

". . . as in the days of her youth" (v. 15) indicates that God will recapitulate his history with Israel, beginning once again his love affair with her in the wilderness. (See the previous discussion under "The Theological Context.")

Vv. 16 and 17 make it clear that Israel has no power within herself to turn from idolatry. God must make turning possible.

V. 18. Sin corrupts our relationships in the realms of both nature and history. Those relationships must therefore be healed in order for Israel to have security in God's new age.

V. 19. Betrothal or engagement was tantamount to marriage in Israel and was a binding commitment, sealed subsequently in marriage by sexual union. In normal practice, the groom paid a bride-price to the father of the bride (cf. Deut. 22:29). Here instead God gives gifts to his bride Israel.

V. 20. "You shall *know* the Lord" is a key phrase in Hosea, signifying the relation of intimate love and faithfulness to God.

Vv. 21-22. God will restore fruitfulness to the land of Canaan.

V. 23. The judgment announced in 1:6, 9 will be reversed, and the covenant relation with Israel restored.

Sermon Possibilities

Numerous possibilities confront the preacher. For example, our enmity with the natural world and its corruption by our sin are frequent themes in Scripture (Gen. 3:15, 17-18; 9:2; Deut. 7:22; Ps. 91:13; Isa. 24:4-5; Jer. 12:4; Hos. 4:1-3; Rom. 8:20-22), but there are probably better passages to use in treating that theme than this one. Similarly, God's destruction of the weapons of war and his gift of peace are motifs throughout the Bible (1 Sam. 2:4; Ps. 46:9; 76:3; Isa. 2:4; 9:5; Mic. 4:3, etc.). Again, other texts afford better opportunities for exposition. The two main principal preaching possibilities from this passage seem to be as follows:

1. The God Who Will Not Give Up on Us

In this text, God is beginning his salvation history with Israel all over again, until she is cleansed of her reliance on the gods and powers of this world and returns in love and faithfulness and knowledge to her divine Husband. Hosea 14 portrays that future return, as do Gomer's restoration to Hosea and its meaning in 3:1-5. The preacher could make mention of both of those passages.

But the question that arises is: *Why* should God try to reclaim his unfaithful bride Israel? Why should he go to all of the trouble of drawing her to himself once again? He tried for years to get her to love and know him. Why bother with her any more? And why should he ceaselessly call his unfaithful church to renewed devotion and try to save her who is equally his bride? Certainly neither Israel nor the new Israel of the church have done anything to deserve such patient and arduous devotion from their Lord.

The answer is manifold and rises solely from the character of God. First, he is the Lord over all, which means that neither Israel's sin nor ours can defeat him. Certainly the empty tomb on Easter morn forever proclaims that fact.

The triumph of God over our evil is not just a matter of his power, however. The text says God pities us (v. 23). In the words of the Psalm for the day, "As a father pities his children, so the Lord pities those who fear him." But even more than that, to those of us who do not fear God, that is, who do not stand in awe of God and who do not obey him: ". . . he knows our frame; he remembers that we are dust." He remembers that we flourish like the flowers of the field and then are gone (Ps. 103:15-16), transient little creatures with no power in ourselves to preserve our own lives. God knows our utter dependence, he pities us in our helplessness, and he works to save us when we cannot save ourselves.

Beyond even his pity, though, God is a God of righteousness and justice; that is, he acts appropriately in his relation with his creatures. He is a God of steadfast, covenant love, who gave his love to his people and who cannot act other than in love, even in judgment. He is a God of mercy, who remembers not wrong, but who wills only right and who removes our sin from us, as far as the East is from the West. He is a God of faithfulness, who does not swerve either from his love or from his goal of making all things and creatures good again. Righteous, just, loving, merciful, faithful — such is the nature of God — and he will act to give all those gifts of character to Israel and to us. The preacher will want to explore in the New Testament how God has accomplished that act.

2. God's Answer to Our Idolatry

We human beings were created to live in relationship with our Creator, which is what it means that we were created in the image of God. We did not choose God any more than we chose the parents to whom we were born. No, God chose us. He chose, when he made us, to create us to be related creatures, dependent always upon him for "our creation, preservation, and all the blessings of this life."

Our primary sin is that we try to escape that relationship. We want to go it on our own. We want to be self-made, self-directed, self-dependent, self-saved masters of our own lives. In short, we want to be our own gods and goddesses. "Come, you can be like God, knowing good and evil," the serpent tells Eve in Genesis 3. We have been trying to be like that since the dawn of time.

We discover in our quest to replace God with self, however, that we do not have the resources within ourselves to nurture and protect our own lives. Consequently we turn to the world to furnish us with the goods of life and with security. We look to manmade gods and human powers to provide our needs and to shield us from the forces and fates that would waste and destroy our lives.

Such was Israel's quest in turning to Baal for vitality and plenty and prosperity, and in "mixing with the nations" (cf. 7:8) for strength and defense. Life with a capital "L," she thought, came from Baal, as we in our time may think maybe it comes from the powers of nature or from mystic realms or from some mythical goddess. Thus Israel and we deny our own created nature as children of our one heavenly Father. We exchange the truth about God for a lie and plunge into idolatry, worshiping and serving the creature rather than the Creator (cf. Rom. 1:25).

God's answer to Israel's idolatry in this Hosea passage is to promise that he will transform Israel. As he did in the beginning, he will speak once more "to her heart" (the Hebrew of 2:14). He will give her a new heart of love and faithfulness (2:19-20), so that she will no longer remember or mention or want to turn to Baal for life, and will never again confuse that pagan deity with her true covenant Lord (2:16-17). As in many of the prophetic writings, the beginning of Israel's salvation will be wrought by a transformation of her character (cf. Jer. 31:33; Ezek. 36:25-27; Zeph. 3:9-13), changing her from an idolatrous harlot into a faithful wife (cf. Hos. 3:5).

Because this is also the church's story, the preacher needs to ask how that transformation of our own faithless character has taken place. And surely Paul's statements in Romans 6 or Galatians 4:19-24 or 2 Corinthians 4:6 have to do with that work of God in our hearts: he "has shone in our hearts to give the light of the knowledge of the glory of God in the face of Christ."

HOSEA 6:1-6

Features to Note in the Text

Following the Septuagint, the RSV connects this passage with 5:15 by the addition of the word "saying." That addition is not in the Hebrew, and 6:1-6 should be interpreted as a separate unit.

The words of the people are quoted in vv. 1-3. The Lord replies in vv. 4-6. The words of the people in vv. 1-3 are not a prayer, however. They speak only to one another, deciding that they need to call a community-wide fast of repentance.

The important word "for" occurs in v. 1 and v. 6. The first occurrence emphasizes that the people speak the words found in vv. 1-3, *because* the Lord has "torn" and "stricken," v. 1. The people's words are their reaction to the loss of much of their land and population to the Assyrian conqueror, Tiglath-pileser III, in 733 B.C. (2 Kings 15:29), following the Syro-Ephraimitic war (2 Kings 16:5-9; Isa. 7:1-9).

The second use of "for," in v. 6, indicates that God's judgment will fall upon Israel *because* of her superficial religiosity.

The passage repeats two key words. First is the "knowledge" of God. The people say they want to "know" him, v. 3. The Lord replies in v. 6 that they have no such "knowledge." Second, God states in v. 4 that Israel's "love" — and the word is *hesed* in the Hebrew, "steadfast covenant love" — is like a transitory morning cloud. But *hesed*, "steadfast love," is exactly what God desires (v. 6).

V. 4. God's reaction to the people's lack of steadfast faithful love and knowledge is not wrath, but searching anguish for some means to save them.

V. 5 indicates that God has brought his judgment on Israel in the past through the action of prophetic words. The understanding of such words is that they are active, effective forces working within Israel to bring about that of which they speak. The Word of God is understood in such a manner throughout the Bible (e.g., cf. Isa. 55:10-11; Ezek. 12:28; 1 Cor. 1:18).

Sermon Possibilities

1. The Desire of God

Our whole life, our destiny, our life or death both now and eternally are determined by what God wants. His is the will being worked out in the historical and natural worlds, and as we know from the New Testament, his is the purpose that will finally be fulfilled. Thus, everything in this passage centers down on those two little words in v. 6, "I desire." What does God desire from Israel and from us?

It is clear that he does not desire superficial worship. Israel exercises what we might call "crisis religiosity" in this passage. She has been devastated by the armies of Assyria. She is in a jam. And so she glibly expects that if she returns to God, he will come to her rescue. God has gone away from her and *returned* to his place (note the verb in the context in 5:15). The remedy is to *return* to the Lord (6:1). Israel here signifies all persons and churches who find themselves in trouble and who suddenly decide to pray for divine help. As we often hear in time of war, "there are no atheists in foxholes."

But God's desire is for steadfast, never-fading faithfulness, for day-after-day commitment to God's will and ways, for step-by-step, day-and-night commitment to one's relationship with the Lord. *Hesed* in vv. 4 and 6 is a covenant term, implying a lifelong fealty. Similarly, "the knowledge of God" involves a daily delight in God's companionship, because one knows his character and action from continual intimate communion with him. In Hosea's figures, it is the knowledge of a faithful wife for her husband, or that of an obedient and adoring son for his father.

In short, that which God desires from Israel is transformation of character — not some urgent prayer when she gets into trouble, not the transitory devotion that lasts just a day or a week, but the lifelong surrender of Israel's heart and soul and mind to her Lord. Worship and prayer have their context in the whole of a person's life, in all they have brought and will bring before God through the years. If the "return" to God is not marked by a turning of the heart and mind, and a redirection of steps and action to follow God's way, it is no return, but simply an empty gesture.

2. False Theology

This passage can also be understood as a telling illustration of Hosea's phrase in 5:4, "They know not the Lord." That is, Israel has a corrupted theology, a distorted understanding of God's nature, a twisted knowledge of who God is. The passage is a good illustration of the importance of sound theology.

Israel believes that God will always forgive her and act favorably toward her. She has merely to go through the motions of worship and of return, and God will come gently and lovingly to her aid, like the gentle rain that fructifies a dry and distressed garden patch.

We see how very closely our lives parallel Israel's, for in our time, many believe that God no longer judges anyone. God is only loving, God is peaceable, God is always forgiving. Like Judah in the time of Jeremiah, we think we can break all the Ten Commandments and then go into the house of the Lord and declare, "We are delivered!" — only to go on doing all of our abominations (Jer. 7:8-10; cf. Mark 11:17). We believe we can go on sinning, in order that grace may abound (Rom. 6:1).

Thus, 5:14 contains words from God that are shocking and unbelievable to us as moderns:

> I will be like a lion to Ephraim,
>   and like a young lion to the house of Judah.
> I, even I, will rend and go away,
>   I will carry off, and none shall rescue.

The fact that God did exactly that in the Assyrian defeat and exile of the ten northern tribes of Israel is something that we simply omit from our theologies. So sin has lost its seriousness for us, and judgment has become an impossibility, and we, like Israel in the time of Hosea, go on doing all of our abominations. Perhaps we need to study anew the admonition in the epistle to the Hebrews, "It is a fearful thing to fall into the hands of the living God" (10:31). Or perhaps it is more convincing to some to listen to the words of Jesus: "Enter by the narrow gate; for the gate is wide and the way is easy that leads to destruction, and those who enter by it are many. For the gate is narrow and the way is hard that leads to life, and those who find it are few" (Matt. 7:13-14).

HOSEA 11:1-11

This passage forms the Old Testament lectionary text for the eighteenth Sunday in Pentecost in Cycle C. It is paired with Colossians 3:1-11 and Luke 12:13-21, which urge us to "seek the things that are above" (Col. 3:1). But it goes very well with the Psalm for the day, Psalm 107:1-9, 43, which is a litany celebrating the steadfast, covenant love of the Lord through years of history.

Features to Note in the Text

Like much of Hosea, the text has been damaged in transmission, and most translations of vv. 2-4, as well as of a few other verses in this passage, rely heavily on the Septuagint, Syriac, and Vulgate, as noted in the footnotes of most Bibles. The RSV is a reliable translation, although the NRSV's rendering of v. 4 is probably to be preferred and is the one we shall use.

V. 1. It is important to note that Israel is adopted as God's son at the time of the exodus from Egypt. This is a familiar concept in the Old Testament (Exod. 4:22-23; Jer. 3:19; 31:20; cf. Deut. 8:5; Isa. 1:2), as is God's fatherhood of Israel (Isa. 63:16; 64:8; Jer. 3:19; 31:9; Mal. 2:10; cf. Isa. 45:11). Matthew 2:15 quotes this verse and applies it to the begotten Son of God, Jesus Christ, whose faithfulness forms a sharp contrast to that of the adopted son Israel.

Vv. 2-3. The Hebrew contains an emphatic contrast owing to the use of separate pronouns. "*They* went from me," v. 2, "But *I* taught Ephraim to walk," v. 3.

V. 4 reads literally in the Hebrew, "I led them with cords of a man," emphasizing God's stooping to the human condition.

There is great emphasis, by the use of repeated verbs, on "turning," "return," "turn." Israel will *return* to Egypt, because they have refused to *return* to God, v. 5. The people are bent on *turning away* from God, v. 7, but God will not *return* to destroy, v. 9 (in the Hebrew). Therefore, after the judgment and exile at the hands of the Assyrian Empire, God will *return* the Israelites to their homes, v. 11.

V. 8. Admah and Zeboim were two of five cities of the plain in the Valley of Sittim at the southern end of the Dead Sea (Gen. 10:19; 14:2). They were destroyed along with Sodom and Gomorrah (Deut. 29:23), a destruction that became a proverbial example of the wrath of God.

V. 8. God weeps at the thought of handing over or giving over his adopted son Israel to death. One of the punishments for sin in the Bible is simply to be loosed or turned over from the guiding and sustaining hand of God and allowed to reap the consequences (Rom. 1:24, 26, 28).

V. 8. It is in God's heart that his grieving over his disobedient son takes place, as also in Genesis 6:6. And his reluctance to give up Israel to death is because of his "compassion," that is, because of totally un-deserved mercy and grace toward his people.

V. 9. God's nature is that he is the "Holy One."

V. 9. Note the threefold repetition of "I will not." God's decision not to destroy is absolutely emphatic.

V. 10 does not accord with the vocabulary of Hosea, and is prob-ably an insert from Amos (cf. Amos 1:2; 3:8). But the thought is con-sonant with the genuine v. 11. On the other side of the judgment, God will return the Israelites to their homes in the promised land.

Sermon Possibilities

The riches of revelation offered to the preacher in this passage are almost beyond number, but we shall note only three of the most important.

1. Israel the Son, God the Father

One often hears the Old Testament characterized as a volume that deals only with legalism and a wrathful God, while the New Testament alone is said to proclaim the love and fatherhood of God. This passage vividly illustrates how false and ill-informed are such stereotypes. The God and Father of our Lord Jesus Christ, who comes to us through the New Testament, is also the God and Father of Israel who is revealed to us through the Old Testament.

God adopts Israel as his son when he redeems Israel from slavery in Egypt. A redeemer, in Israelite thought, was a *family member,* who bought back a relative who had fallen into slavery (cf. Levit. 25:47-55). By delivering Israel in the exodus, God was thus declaring that Israel belonged to his family. Israel was his adopted son who could not be abandoned to affliction and suffering (cf. Exod. 3:7), his child who could not be left to die in a strange land.

Israel had done nothing to deserve such attentive love, having as yet obeyed no law and worked no piety. Israel did not even know the name of God at this point (cf. Exod. 3:13). God simply chose Israel to be his people, set his love upon them, redeemed them, and freed them for a new life, in the glorious liberty of the children of God. As Moses says to Israel, "It was not because you were more in number than any other people that the Lord set his love upon you and chose you, for you were the fewest of all peoples; but it is because the Lord loves you . . ." (Deut. 7:7). Pure, undeserved love!

It is that image that Paul uses, then, to speak in Galatians 4:3-7 of our redemption by Jesus Christ. We too were slaves, Paul says, to "the elemental spirits of the universe," to sin and to the wages of sin that is death (Rom. 6:23). But through Jesus Christ, God adopted us as his children and redeemed us out of our slavery. Long before we had done anything to deserve it, long before we had worked any obedience of faith, "while we were yet sinners Christ died for us" (Rom. 5:8). Out of pure, undeserved love! And so now we, like Israel, can call God our Father (Gal. 4:6; Rom. 8:15), because the Spirit of God has been poured into our hearts (Rom. 5:5; 8:9; 2 Cor. 3:17).

Further, it was when the Israelites were redeemed from bondage that they became a people and could therefore be named by the corporate title "son." Before their deliverance, they were a "mixed multitude" (cf. Exod. 12:38), from various tribes and backgrounds. But when they were set free, they became one people, God's covenant people, and the one tie that united them was that they had all been redeemed together. If they forgot what God had done for them, they became "no people" (Hos. 1:9). Thus, our passage reminds the Israelites of God's redemption of them. "When Israel was a child, I loved him, and out of Egypt I called my son" (v. 1).

So it is, too, that the church is a "mixed multitude" of all sorts of races and backgrounds. And the one tie that binds us together as a universal community is the fact that we have all been redeemed together. By our redemption through the cross of Jesus Christ, we have become one people, God's adopted children. But if we forget that redemption, we too become "no people" (1 Pet. 2:10) and our unity becomes impossible.

This passage can be preached, not only to reveal to a congregation God's undeserved love in adopting them into his family, but also to point them to the one real basis of their identity and common fellowship, community, and unity.

2. The Walking Lesson

Nowhere in the Scriptures is there a more poignant portrayal of God. "It was I who taught Ephraim to walk." That is the Lord of heaven and earth speaking, the God who can measure the oceans in the hollow of his hand (Isa. 40:12), before whom the nations are like a drop in a bucket (Isa. 40:15), who can make the rulers of the earth as nothing (Isa. 40:23), and to whom nothing and no one can be compared (Isa. 40:25). "Yet it was I who taught Ephraim to walk" — God the Father bending down to offer a supporting finger to the unsteady, toddling infant Israel; letting him fall at times; encouraging his little steps; praising him when he does well; and then sweeping him up in his arms when he starts to cry (v. 3), wiping away his tears, and comforting him against his cheek (v. 4 NRSV).

All of God's patient, tender, forgiving, guiding fatherhood is revealed in that portrayal. God has taught Israel how to walk — guiding his son with words of law and prophets and priests. He has repeatedly forgiven the child when he has stumbled or deliberately run away. God has constantly comforted his son when the child has been injured or disappointed or despairing. All of these images reflect the historical actions of God toward Israel as they are recorded in the Old Testament. And all of them reflect the historical actions of God toward the church. If the preacher will use Hosea's imagery, great power can be lent to the proclamation of what God has done for us, both as individuals and as the church.

3. The God Who Must Be God

Verse 9 is crucial in this passage. God is "the Holy One." When used of God, the term "holy" is the description of his divinity, and it signifies that God is totally Other, unlike anyone or anything in heaven or on earth. He cannot be equated with the numinous powers found in nature or with any spirit found in human beings. He works in both nature and human lives, but he is not identical with any of them. He is totally God, totally different, totally himself and no other, known to us only as he reveals himself in his words and actions in the history of Israel and supremely in our Lord Jesus Christ.

This Holy God, however, is revealed through the witness of Hosea to grieve over his disobedient children — both Israel and us — and to love us with a "love divine, all loves excelling."[4] Despite anything Israel or we have done or left undone, despite the fact that we have repeatedly gone away from our Father (v. 2), God loves us. His holy nature is love, beyond all other loves, and so he loves us, despite ourselves. As John says of Jesus, "having loved his own who were in the world, he loved them to the end" (John 13:1), even when they denied and deserted him and he hung upon a cross for their sakes and ours.

But this God who is pure love is also Lord of all, and if his children should successfully defy that lordship, God would not be their Lord. So Israel, according to our passage, will be appointed to the yoke of Assyria (v. 5), and their ten northern tribes will be lost in exile. And those of us who prefer to be our own gods and goddesses will be lost in death. The lordship of God cannot be mocked. We will reap what we have sown (Gal. 6:7). And yet, and yet, "all Israel will be saved" (Rom. 11:26), and finally sinful humanity will bow every knee and confess with every tongue before its Lord Jesus Christ (Phil. 2:10-11). In the mysterious power and love of God, sin and disobedience will not win the final victory. The resurrection of Christ beyond the cross is testimony to that fact. God who is Love beyond all love will bring his children to his good conclusion. "How can I give you up, Ephraim? How can I hand you over, Israel?" . . . "I will not come to destroy." The Lord God, the Holy One of Israel in our midst, has come to save, and save he will beyond all our just deserts, and beyond all ways of human reckoning.

Since all of these things will come to pass, what sort of persons

---

4. The first words of the hymn by Charles Wesley.

should we be (2 Pet. 3:11)? A spoiled and rebellious child will not fit very well into an eternal family of God's that is characterized by love. In fact, such a child may feel as if he is living in eternal hell.

In the history of Israel, this passage takes on eschatological dimensions, for it is finally only beyond the destruction and loss of Israel to the Assyrian Empire that God fulfills these words of Hosea. His promises here are made sure by the death and resurrection of Christ. And the hope of eternal salvation toward which we and Israel press lies finally only in the love of God. That love will triumph. How and why remains hidden in the Holy One.

Preaching from the Book of Joel

Recommended Commentaries

Elizabeth Achtemeier. *Minor Prophets I.* New International Biblical
    Commentary. Peabody, Mass: Hendrickson Press, 1996.
Hans Walter Wolff. *Joel and Amos.* Hermeneia. Philadelphia: Fortress
    Press, 1977.

The Historical Context

As is not the case with some of the other prophetic books, the historical
context of Joel is largely immaterial to its interpretation.

The book was written in the quiet, postexilic time between 500
and 350 B.C., when Judah had long been a tiny subprovince of the Persian
Empire. Priests and elders, rather than kings and princes, are leaders of
the postexilic congregation, and the existence of the second temple,
which was completed in 515 B.C., is taken for granted.

Sometime during that century and a half, Judah experienced a
devastating locust plague which literally stripped her land bare of every
shred of vegetation (1:4-10). Just when the land was beginning to re-
cover, a drought withered the new growth (1:11-12, 16-20). It is following the locust plague and during the drought that the prophet Joel
delivers his message.

The Theological Context

Two theological emphases dominate the book of Joel — the Day of the Lord and repentance. Though the prophecies begin with an account of the locust plague and of a drought, those devastations are but harbingers of a greater catastrophe yet to come that will involve not only Judah but the cosmos as a whole. "The day of the Lord is near, and as destruction from the Almighty it comes" (1:15).

Joel is given to see by God — not by the locust plague, but by a revelation from God — that God's final judgment day is approaching. Judah stands in mortal danger, because of her sin against the Lord, and the sign of her separation from God is the fact that she has no more grain, wine, and oil with which to carry out the daily sacrifices in the temple (1:9-10; cf. 2:14, 19, 24). Her communion with her Lord is no more.

Joel never spells out what Judah's sin is. But Joel's name means "Ja [a shortened form of Jahweh, Lord] is God," and at two crucial points in the book, it is asserted that God's actions will cause Judah to know that the Lord (Jahweh) is God (2:27; 3:17). Judah's sin is therefore apparently that of apostasy, of devotion to other gods and goddesses.

The Day of the Lord comes, with its darkness and gloom, its clouds and thick darkness, its devouring fire, and its mysterious destroying Foe from the north, which is the armies of God (2:1-11; cf. 2:20). Based on her experience of God's battles for her in the time of the Judges, Israel had earlier thought that the Day of the Lord would be the time when God would defeat all her enemies and exalt her among the nations in his kingdom. Amos and the prophets who succeeded him disabused Israel of such happy thoughts (Amos 5:18-20; Zeph. 1; Isa. 2:6-22; Ezek. 7; Mal. 4:5; 3:1-5). Because of her sin, Israel would be subjected to the burning fire of God's judgment along with all the nations. Chapter 3 of Joel vividly pictures that judgment on all nations, just as Joel 2:28-32 portrays the events that will precede it.

Against the background of the prophecy of the coming of the day of final judgment, the second great intonation in Joel's prophecies sounds — the call to repentance (2:12-17). Even in the face of Judah's apostasy, and despite the fact that the covenant curses of locust plague and drought have come upon her because of her unfaithfulness (cf. Deut. 28:23-24, 38-42), God through his prophet utters a "Yet — even now" (2:12). There is still room for repentance and return, if it is sincere repentance from the heart (2:12-14)! Therefore the prophet bids the priests to lead the people in that communal fast of penitence (2:15-17).

The promises of salvation that follow in 2:18-27 are not God's automatic reaction to Judah's repentance, however (cf. 2:14). They issue out of the character of God (cf. 2:13), who in his compassion for his people is determined to fulfill his worldwide purposes through them (2:18).

JOEL 2:12-17

This passage is the stated lesson for Ash Wednesday in all three cycles of the three-year lectionary. It is paired with Romans 13:11-14 in year A; 1 Corinthians 1:3-9 in Year B; and 1 Thessalonians 3:9-13 in Year C; and all of those passages in the epistles deal with the coming Day of the Lord. Similarly, all three Gospel lessons, Matthew 24:36-44; Mark 13:24-37; and Luke 21:25-36, are taken from Jesus' apocalyptic sayings concerning the coming of the Son of Man. The church has always connected Christ's second coming with the final judgment on the Day of the Lord, when he returns to set up his kingdom on earth.

Features to Note in the Text

God speaks in vv. 12-13a, the prophet takes up the speech in v. 13b and furnishes a prayer for the priest to utter in v. 17.

V. 12. The verse begins with an adversative *waw* in the Hebrew — "but" or "yet" — to form a strong contrast, a reversal, to that which has preceded it.

Vv. 12-14. The word "hearts" occurs twice (vv. 12, 13), emphasizing the inward and sincere repentance called for.

"Return" is found in all three verses. Both the Lord and the prophet issue the imperative to "return" (vv. 12, 13). It may be that the Lord will then "return" to his people.

The important word "for" occurs in v. 13, giving the reason why return to the Lord is possible. It is because he is "gracious and merciful, slow to anger, abounding in steadfast [covenant] love," and willing to take back his planned judgment on his people. Such a characterization of God's nature is found throughout the Old Testament (Exod. 34:6-7; Num. 14:18; Neh. 9:17; Ps. 86:15; 103:8; 145:8; Jon. 4:2; Nah. 1:3).

"Jahweh your God" is repeated (vv. 13, 14), emphasizing the one who alone is Judah's God.

Rending of garments, "fasting, weeping, and mourning" (vv. 12-13) are all characteristic of communal fasts of lamentation, such as that called for in vv. 15-17. Such fasts were held whenever Israel was in any sort of trouble from war, famine, or pestilence. They were an opportunity for communal repentance and were characterized by expressions of sorrow for sin before God. They included also prostrations on the ground, beating of breasts, putting of ashes upon the head (from which comes our practice of marking with ashes on Ash Wednesday). Normal activities ceased; no one was excluded from the ceremony, as is clear in v. 16.

"Cereal offering" and "drink offering" (v. 14) were necessary for daily sacrifice and communion with God in the temple.

Preaching Possibilities

1. Yet, Even Now

"We shall all stand before the judgment seat of God," writes Paul (Rom. 14:10). Throughout its pages, the New Testament proclaims that the Day of the Lord is coming — that Day when Christ will return to set up the Kingdom of God, and when there will be a final judgment as to who will inherit eternal life in the kingdom and who will not (cf. the Gospel readings for Ash Wednesday). No one knows when that Day will come, Jesus teaches, neither he nor the angels, but only the Father (Mark 13:32 and parallels).

Jesus' admonition, therefore, is "Watch!" Be ready! (cf. Matt. 25). For God is not mocked, and what we have sown, we shall also reap (Gal. 6:7-9). Paul's constant prayer for his churches is that they will be found guiltless and blameless on the Day of the Lord and thus be able to stand before the judgment (cf. the epistle lessons).

Those are fearful tidings, for as Joel says, "The Day of the Lord is great and very terrible; who can endure it?" (Joel 2:11). Not one of us has done anything to make us worthy to inherit eternal life in the Kingdom of God.

But into our fearful and sinful situation God speaks this word of good news, of the gospel, through his prophet Joel. "Yet even now." Even now, in twentieth-century America and in all the years to come; even now, in the midst of our violent, unjust, unbelieving, indifferent society; even now, in our situation, marked as we are with disdain for our neighbors' needs and neglect of the will of our God; even now, in the midst of our fears, our sufferings, our guilts, and our ignorance, the God of all mercy holds out to us the opportunity for repentance and return, that we may stand and know salvation in the Day of the Lord.

By the outstretched arms of our Savior on the cross, we are assured that the way of return is open. There forgiveness is offered to us, no matter what our situation. There, now, even now, we may find the mercy that allows us to return to our God.

2. Rend Your Hearts

The Bible knows so well the source of our sin — in our evil hearts. It is in the "imagination of the thoughts of our hearts," says Genesis (6:5), that our wickedness lodges — our grudges, our prides, our hatreds, our selfishness. What comes out of a person's heart is what defiles him or her, Jesus teaches (Mark 7:20-23) — "evil thoughts, fornication, theft, murder, adultery, coveting, wickedness, deceit, licentiousness, envy, slander, pride, foolishness."

Thus the prophets call for repentance, turning, change in our hearts. "Circumcise yourselves to the Lord, remove the foreskin of your hearts," Jeremiah pleads (4:4). "Get yourselves a new heart and a new spirit! Why will you die?" Ezekiel questions (18:31). Love the Lord with all your heart, commands Moses, and let his words be upon your heart (Deut. 6:4-6). And here in Joel, the imperative is "Rend your hearts and not your garments." That is, repent, not by outward show of penitence and sorrow, as in Israel's fast of repentance. But repent with a heart broken and sorrowful over your sin, because "a broken and contrite heart, O God, thou wilt not despise" (Ps. 51:17).

The presupposition is that heart-rending repentance will lead to new action, that out of the heart there will flow goodness, kindness, peace, love, justice, and righteousness. For "to repent" in biblical thought is to turn around, to go in the opposite direction, to change the direction of one's life-walk. And if the change has not been made, there has been no true repentance.

Certainly the new life of true repentance involves the will, the determination to get out of bed every morning and to be obedient to God's commands, the silent taking oneself in hand and following, step by step, the way of our Lord. "Work out your own salvation with fear and trembling," Paul writes (Phil. 2:12).

But the quotation from Paul continues, "For God is at work in you, both to will and to work for his good pleasure." And that is the final assurance when it comes to rending our hearts. God not only commands that we repent and change in our hearts, but he gives us the power to do so. The promise is there in Jeremiah's new covenant — that covenant that our Lord made with us when he sat at table at the Last Supper: "I will put my law within in them, and I will write it upon their hearts," God vows (Jer. 31:33). And the promise is in Ezekiel's prophecy, too:

> A new heart I will give you, and a new spirit I will put within you; and I will take out of your flesh the heart of stone and give you a heart of flesh. And I will put my spirit within you, and cause you to walk in my statutes and be careful to observe my ordinances. (Ezek. 36:26-27)

So it is that Paul can declare that the prophetic promises have been fulfilled and that "God's love has been poured into our hearts through the Holy Spirit which has been given to us" (Rom. 5:5). The very Spirit of his Son has been sent into our hearts to allow us to call God "Father" once more and to enter into his presence as beloved children and heir of all his promises (Gal. 4:6-7).

Joel's call to rend our hearts comes to us therefore as the only way of true repentance. But we have the assurance of the gospel that through faith in Christ, that repentant new life will be wrought in us by his Spirit poured into our hearts (cf. Rom 6:17; 2 Cor. 1:22; 4:6; Eph. 3:17; Col. 3:15).

JOEL 2:28-32

This is the stated lectionary text for Pentecost 30C in the three-year lectionary. It is paired with the parable of the Pharisee and publican or tax-collector, found in Luke 18:9-14, and with the statements concerning Paul's faithfulness and expectation of final reward, in 2 Timothy 4:6-8, 16-18. Thus, both of the paired passages are emphasizing what it means, in Joel 2:32, to call on the name of the Lord.

Features to Note in the Text

As is evident from the word "before" in v. 31, the passage concerns those events that will take place preceding the Day of the Lord, the final day of judgment.

"I will pour out my spirit" occurs in both v. 28 and v. 29. While v. 28 says the spirit will be granted to "all flesh," the repeated use of "your" in v. 28 limits the gift of the spirit to Judah. However, the passage is quoted by Peter in Acts 2:17-21 to explain the gift of the spirit at Pentecost, and there the bounds of Judah are sprung to give the gift of the spirit a universal dimension.

In v. 32 it is stated that those who call on the name of the Lord will be saved in the final judgment, but at the end of that verse, the saved remnant is further described as "those whom the Lord calls." God's is the prior act.

Sermon Possibilities

1. The Gift of the Spirit

There is great confusion in the church about the nature of the Holy Spirit. Throughout the Bible, the Spirit is the activity and presence of God within human life. In Christian Trinitarian terms, the Holy Spirit is the third person of the Godhead, fully equivalent to the Father and the Son, at one with them, and continuing their work and presence in our lives. Thus, in Romans 8:9-11, Paul can use "Spirit," "Spirit of God," and "Spirit of Christ" interchangeably. And in John 14:18, Jesus promises that he will not leave his followers "desolate," but will come to them in the person of the Spirit. It follows, therefore, that the nature of the Spirit must always be understood as consonant with the portrayal of both the Father and the Son that we have in the Scriptures. The Spirit never speaks or acts contrary to Christ or to the nature of his Father.

This passage in Joel promises that God will pour out his Spirit on "all flesh," and that becomes a gift to every Christian at the time of his or her baptism (Acts 2:37-38). The result is that every Christian now can enjoy the intimate relation with God known to the prophets of old — which is the meaning of vv. 28c-29. Here, before the final judgment on the Day of the Lord, we have the assurance that we can be brought into fellowship with our Lord by means of his gift of his Spirit.

2. How Can We Be Saved in the Final Judgment?

Joel tells us that having been given the gift of the Spirit of God, we are to use the gift! We are to use it to "call on the name of the Lord." That means we are not only to worship God, as in Genesis 12:8, but we are to depend always on God for our very lives and good. When the day of judgment comes, it is not those who suddenly turn to God in desperate attempts to save their own skins who will be spared. Rather it is those who, throughout their days, have seen in God their one security and way (cf. Isa. 12:2-4; Matt. 7:21-23; 25:31-46).

But it is *his* name on which we are to call. Only the God of the Scriptures, fully and finally revealed to us in Jesus Christ, can offer us that sure salvation. He is the Lord and no other (cf. Phil 2:10-11; cf. Isa. 45:22-23). We call on him, on his name, or we cannot call at all. The petty powers and useless godlets of this world have no refuge to offer us. "For there is no other name under heaven given among men [and women] by which we can be saved" (Acts 4:12).

Finally, to call on the name of the Lord means also to tell others what he has done (Ps. 105:1; Isa. 12:2-4), to be his witnesses throughout the earth (Acts 1:8). This is the task that Paul has in mind when he quotes Joel 2:32 in Romans 10:13. How can persons call on the name of the Lord when they have never heard of his deeds and words? And how can they hear without someone to tell them? So those who have been given the Spirit of God are to tell others the glorious good news — that others too may be saved, that others too may escape God's final judgment on their lives and enter into his eternal kingdom, through the forgiveness and love of God shown forth in Jesus Christ our Lord.

Preaching from the Book of Amos

Recommended Commentaries

Elizabeth Achtemeier. *Minor Prophets I.* New International Bible Commentary. Peabody, Mass: Hendrickson Publishers, 1996.

John Calvin. *Commentaries on the Twelve Minor Prophets, II.* Joel, Amos, Obadiah. Edinburgh: The Calvin Translation Society, 1896.

James Luther Mays. *Amos.* Old Testament Library. Philadelphia: The Westminster Press, 1969.

Hans Walter Wolff. *Joel and Amos.* Hermeneia. Philadelphia: Fortress Press, English translation, 1977.

The Historical Context

Amos was the first of those writing prophets whose oracles we have preserved for us in the Old Testament. His ministry took place around the year 760 B.C., when Jeroboam II (787/6-747/6) was on the throne of the northern kingdom of Israel. The Assyrian Empire was the dominant military power at the time, but it was occupied with advances of the kingdom of Urartu from Asia Minor. Thus Jeroboam was free to expand his territory and to enrich his economy with lively trade and commerce. The result was a growing upper class luxuriating in opulence (Amos 6:4-6) but totally indifferent to the plight of the poor. While engaging in elaborate but superficial cultic practices (4:4-5; 5:21-23), the rich increased their wealth by expropriating the land of poor debtors or by subjecting them to slavery (2:6; 8:4, 6), denying the helpless any justice in the law courts (2:7; 5:10, 12) and cheating them in the market-place (8:5). Conspicuous consumption (4:1), debauchery (6:5-6), and immorality characterized their lifestyle. It was this situation that Amos addressed.

The Theological Context

Contrary to an oft-repeated stereotype, Amos was not a poor peasant from the south, whose words resulted from his shock over the northern kingdom's practices. Rather, Amos was a wealthy sheep-breeder (*nōqēd*, cf. 2 Kings 3:4) and an owner of sycamore fig orchards in the lowlands around the Dead Sea and along the Mediterranean coast (7:14). His home was in Tekoa in Judah, some ten miles south of Jerusalem, but he was summoned by God temporarily to leave his business and to go to the northern kingdom to preach (7:15; 3:8) — a summons that Amos could not resist. Thus the content of his preaching came not from his own evaluation of the northern situation, but from the revelations given him by God. Probably his ministry lasted a few short years, whereupon he returned to his home and occupation.

The context of all the words that the Lord gave Amos to speak is God's covenant with his people Israel. Israel was God's elected people (3:2), his "own possession" (Exod. 19:5), whom the Lord delivered out of Egypt, guided for forty years through the wilderness, and to whom he gave the promised land and prophets and Nazarites to guide their life (Amos 2:9-11). Israel's purpose in the world was to be God's "kingdom of priests and a holy nation" (Exod. 19:4-6), set apart for God's purpose alone, to mediate the knowledge of God to the rest of the world. Incumbent upon Israel, therefore, was obedience to God's covenant demands for righteousness and justice within her society and for sincere worship of his lordship. By such practices Israel would honor the name of Adonai Yahweh Sebaoth (the Lord God of hosts; 3:13; 4:13; 5:3, 8, 16, 27; 6:8, 14; 7:1; 8:3; 9:5, 6), in obedience to the third commandment of the covenant Decalogue.

Northern Israel, however, rejected the Lord's covenant commands and joined the rest of the nations of the ancient Near East in their common rebellion against the lordship of God (1:1–2:16). Amos was therefore commanded to preach the terrifying message that God in his judgment would make a complete end of the northern kingdom (5:17;

7:8-9; 8:2; 9:1-4), a prophecy that was fulfilled when the ten northern tribes were conquered and deported in 721 B.C. by the Assyrian Empire and disappeared from history. Israel's rebellion against her covenant lord was absolute. It therefore could be done away only by totally wiping it out. In the final judgment of her life, on the Day of the Lord (5:18-20; 8:9-10), Israel would be destroyed (9:8b). (Any thought of a remnant, as in 9:8c, is secondary to Amos's preaching.)

AMOS 3:1-2

Features to Note in the Text

The prophet speaks in v. 1. Verse 2 is then a direct quote of the Lord's word.

The "word" of v. 1 is "against" Israel, that is, it is a word of judgment on her life.

The word is directed against not only the northern kingdom, but against "the whole family which I brought up out of the land of Egypt." That is, it is directed against the whole of the covenant people, the whole company of those who enjoy the benefits of God's redemption. Thus, it is a word spoken also to the church, which Paul calls "the Israel of God" (Gal. 6:16) and an heir by faith of the promises to Abraham (Gal. 3:9; 4:7).

The passage follows immediately on 1:1–2:16 and must be read in that context. The two opening chapters of Amos's prophecies are intended to show how Israel has joined the other nations in common rebellion against the Lord. Rather than being a people separated out from the nations as God's elected instrument (cf. Num. 23:9), Israel has become like all the others. Their sin is also hers.

Sermon Possibilities

1. The Story We Have in Common

Throughout the Scriptures, Israel is the elected, chosen people of God, set apart by the Lord to be used in his purpose of bringing blessings on all the families of the earth (Gen. 12:3; Exod. 19:5-6; Rom. ch. 11, esp. vv. 28-29). But through the work of Jesus Christ, the church has inherited that role. The same electing words of Exodus 19:5-6 that God spoke to Israel at Mt. Sinai are spoken to the church in 1 Peter 2:9-10. Grafted into the root of Israel (Rom. 11:17-24), joined to her commonwealth (Eph. 2:11-22), we have become members of God's elected people, solely "known" by him among "all the families of the earth."

That does not mean that God does not work in the lives and histories of other peoples. Of course he does. Amos points that out in his first two chapters as well as in 9:7. It also does not mean that we and Israel were chosen simply for privilege. Israel recognizes in the story of Jacob that her election costs her struggle and wounding (Gen. 32:22-31), just as the election of the church has cost her countless martyrs for the faith (Hebr. 11:32-38; 1 Pet.; Rev.), and the numberless struggles of everyday disciples.

Rather, both Israel and the church were elected by God for a task — to be his witnesses (Isa. 43:10, 12; 44:8) to the ends of the earth (Acts 1:8). Israel was to tell all peoples what God had done for her salvation, that all nations would say, "Let us go with you, for we have heard that God is with you" (Zech. 8:23). The church is to go into all the world, declaring the wonderful deeds of him who called it out of darkness into his marvelous light (1 Pet. 2:10) — making disciples, baptizing them in the name of the Triune God, teaching them the commandments of the Lord (Matt. 20:28).

That was the purpose of Israel's election, and it is the purpose of ours — the meaning of our lives — until the kingdom comes and every knee bows and every tongue confesses that Jesus Christ is Lord (Phil. 2:11; cf. Isa. 45:23).

2. The Uniqueness of God's People

Election means being set apart by God for his purpose, and so the Israel of the Old Testament and the church cannot live the way the rest of the world lives, doing as the society around them does. Israel was forbidden to follow the ways of Egypt or of Canaan; she had to live by the Lord's ordinances (Levit. 18:1-4), which she promised at Sinai to do (Exod. 19:8; 24:3). And the church cannot be conformed to this world, but must always act according to the will of God, which is given to the church through the Scriptures and which is good and acceptable and perfect (Rom. 12:2; cf. Matt. 13:22; Gal. 1:4; 1 Pet. 1:14-15; 1 John 2:15).

Israel and the church are not "natural" people, bound together by ties of blood or soil or economic interest, and so they cannot do just what comes naturally; it is not natural to love your enemies or to die for someone who hates you. It is the custom of society to return evil for evil, or to despise the poor and weak, or to look out for number one. "But a new commandment I give to you, that you love one another." Pray for those who persecute you. Blessed are the poor. The meek shall inherit the earth. Whoever saves his life shall lose it. Everywhere throughout the Scriptures, God's will is not the world's will, and his thoughts and ways are not society's. And Israel and the church are bound to him by love and covenant and promise.

3. Judgment on God's Elect

In our text, precisely because Israel is the elected people of God, he will punish her for all her iniquities. That is a word also to the church. It is not only the promises of salvation in the Old Testament that apply to the church. So too do the promises of judgment. We therefore need to understand the purpose of God's judgments.

The God of the Bible is not an avenging, punishing God, who zaps his people whenever they stray from his will. That is an unfortunate and erroneous stereotype laid upon the God of the Scriptures. Rather, this God of Israel and Father of our Lord Jesus Christ is a restless, moving, always active Lord who is working toward a goal. He is working toward the time when he can, as he promised Abraham, bring his blessing on all the families of the earth (Gen. 12:3). He is working to restore his creation to the goodness he intended for it in the beginning (Gen. 1:31). We corrupted every aspect of God's creation, as Genesis 3–11 tells us. Now God unceasingly works to erase that corruption, and to bring in a time when death shall be no more, and there is neither mourning nor pain nor crying any more and God himself can dwell in our midst (Rev. 21:3-4), a holy God in the midst of a transformed and holy people.

Amazingly, Israel and the church and you and I have been chosen by God to be his instruments in accomplishing that loving purpose. But when we disobey his will, given us in the Scriptures, when we forget his redemption and mercy and turn to other goals and deities, we become not useful instruments, but obstacles to God's purpose.

What is God to do? He will fulfill his promises. His kingdom *will* come on earth, even as it is in heaven. He would not be the Lord of heaven and earth if that were not so. Obviously, he could just brush us aside and go on with his work — initially that is what happened to Israel. But this amazing God of love promises a final salvation of Israel (cf. Rom. 11:26), and he does not discard us as useless. Rather, by his temporal judgments, he tries to correct us.

Sometimes these are the judgments of every day, as Amos proclaims (4:6-11) — in Isaiah's words, "here a little, there a little" (28:13) — all in the effort to get us to return to him. And so we experience anxieties and sufferings and disruptions of our lives, broken relationships and broken hearts, *some* of which are surely the judgments of God upon us.

But God is working to cleanse us, transform us, renew us. He knows that he cannot pour new wine into old wineskins, that he cannot sew new patches on old garments (Matt. 9:16-17), that our old faithless ways must be done away with — die — before we can bring forth fruit for his purpose (John 12:24). So God "prunes" us (John 15:2), pounds us (Jer. 18:1-4), disciplines us (Deut. 8:5; Hebr. 12:6, 10), judges us, to remake us into instruments fit to further his purpose of blessing and love for the world. In his judgment, God could throw us away. In his mercy, he does not do so. He transforms us.

AMOS 5:14-15

Features to Note in the Text

This brief admonition is set in the wider context of 5:1-17, which begins (v. 2) and ends (v. 16) with a funeral dirge pronounced over sinful Israel. God's people are as good as dead, because of their idolatrous worship (v. 5) and their injustice in their courts of law (vv. 10, 12, 15) and toward their poor debtors (v. 11).

The two imperatives, "seek good" and "hate evil," are defined by the context. To seek good is to seek the Lord, as is clear in vv. 4 and 6. To hate evil is to hate idolatry and injustice.

The only hope of escaping death is conditional ("it may be," v. 15), dependent not on human action but on the grace of God. God is free to save whom he will (Cf. Exod. 33:19; Luke 17:10).

Sermon Possibility

1. What Is Good?

We live in a society in which there is no longer an agreed upon definition of "good." Each person defines the good solely in individualistic terms of "what is good for *me*." Good and evil, right and wrong have become totally relative to the individual's desires within any particular situation. No objective standard of good lies beyond the individual, and certainly there is no striving in our society to be good, according to some objective measure. Goodness in that sense is out of fashion. And any thought of what the church calls "sanctification," growing up into the goodness of Christ, has fallen out of use.

The Scriptures, however, know what is good. Micah 6:8 says God has shown human beings what is good — to do justice, and love faithfulness (*ḥeseḏ*), and to walk humbly with God. Amos, in this passage, reflects those goals — justice toward the helpless, covenant faithfulness to God, sincere worship of him alone.

But finally to "seek good" is to seek God, as in vv. 4 and 6 of Amos 5:1-17, for God alone is the source of goodness. "Why do you call me good?" Jesus asked. "No one is good but God alone" (Mark 10:18). Goodness is God's nature. What he does is good. What he commands is good, and there is no other standard of good lying outside of him.

Thus to do good works is to do them in relation to God, and that which is not done for him and in him is not good — a teaching profoundly set forth in Matthew 25:40, 45. We may think some atheist is a virtuous person, doing all sorts of humanitarian good works. But no. Unless our works honor God, obey God, point to God, arise out of our love for God, they are not good (cf. Matt. 5:16). We were created "to glorify God and enjoy him forever," says the Shorter Catechism. That is the purpose of our living. Israel apart from God cannot be good. And neither can we. And of course it is because we always fall short of acting and living to the glory of God (cf. Luke 17:10) that Jesus Christ must atone for our lack and fill out our goodness.

AMOS 5:21-24

These verses form a part of the section, Amos 5:18–6:14, which deals with Israel's deluded confidence that no harm will come upon her from God. She is wealthy (6:1-7) and so she feels that God's favor rests upon her. She is militarily strong (6:8-14) and she relies on that might. She looks forward to the Day of the Lord (5:18-20), when she believes God will defeat all of her enemies and exalt her over the nations. And she thinks that her lavish cult sustains God's approval and protection of her (5:21-24).

Most of the prophets attack Israel's worship practices (cf. Isa. 1:10-17; 58; Jer. 7:1-15; Mal. 1:6-14, et al.), not because the prophets prefer purely spiritual worship to sacrificial ritual, but because Israel's worship is empty show, unmatched by sincere love for God and faithful obedience to his will.

Features to Note in the Text

The description in this passage of Israel's worship is quite comprehensive. "Feasts" (v. 21) refers to the three principal pilgrimage festivals to Bethel or Gilgal of Tabernacles, Passover, and Unleavened Bread. "Solemn assemblies" (v. 21) indicates sabbaths, new moons, and other less important occasions. In addition, the major types of sacrifice are listed — "burnt offerings"; "cereal offerings," which could be of any type; and "peace offerings," which emphasized communion with God and with fellow Israelites and which were often accompanied by singing to the music of a lute (or harp).

Three verbs are used to describe the Lord's rejection of Israel's worship. "I will not accept them," v. 22, is literally, "I will not smell them." "I will not look upon," v. 22, and "I will not listen," v. 23. Thus, God closes his nostrils, his eyes, and his ears to Israel's worship of him (cf. Isa. 1:15). He rejects it all.

"Justice" in this passage refers to the establishment of God's order within the orders of society. "Righteousness" refers to the fulfillment of those demands that God decrees in relationships with family and neighbors and fellow citizens and strangers.

Sermon Possibility

1. The Inseparable Pair

As the Epistle of 1 John states, "If any one says, 'I love God,' and hates his brother, he is a liar; for he who does not love his brother whom he has seen, cannot love God whom he has not seen" (1 John 4:20). Love for God, manifested in praise and prayer in our worship, must be matched by love for our neighbors, manifested in deeds of justice and righteousness toward all. The two loves are inseparable, as our Lord pointed out when he spoke of the two greatest commandments (Mark 12:28-31 and parallels).

Thus, in Amos's time, Israel cannot properly worship God or count on his favor toward them when they are disobeying God's will by subjecting the poor and helpless to injustice in their courts and commerce. It is a truth that should give every worshiper in our time cause to tremble. Are even our individual prayers heard by God, or are they rejected, as Isaiah 1:15 says, because we have blood on our hands?

To be sure, we do not work our way into God's favor or earn our deliverance and salvation at his hands. He redeems and will save us for his eternal kingdom solely out of the pure grace of his mercy and love toward us. In the end, that is the reason he will save Israel too, and neither Israel nor we are ever worthy of that salvation.

But we can turn our back on God by turning our back on our fellow human beings whom God loves and to whom he has sent us to minister in his name. We can walk away from the love and mercy that God would show us by walking away from our needy neighbors. We can reject the eternal salvation that God would freely give us. To reject others is to reject our Lord (Matt. 25:41-46). Worship and practice cannot be separated.

AMOS 7:1-6

I wish to comment only briefly on these two visions, discussing not their place in the total message of Amos or their import for the fate of Israel, but simply three implications for our lives today.

Features to Note in the Text

The prophets of the Old Testament sometimes experienced ecstatic states in which they were granted visions of what God was going to do in the future. Amos has five such visions, recounted in 7:1-9; 8:1-3; and 9:1-4; Isaiah, Jeremiah, Ezekiel, Second Isaiah, Habakkuk, and Zechariah all experience them, as does Elisha earlier.

Amos's visions in this passage are of a judgment of locusts which the Lord is about to loose on Israel in the late spring, and of a judgment of the fire of God's wrath to be loosed in the summer.

In reaction to the visions, Amos intercedes before God for his sinful people, praying first that God will forgive the people (v. 2), but then asking that God will halt his judging action (v. 5). Such intercession was a standard, if little remarked, feature of the prophetic office, exercised first by Moses (Deut. 9:17-20, 25-29), and then by Jeremiah (7:16-17; 11:14; 15:1), Ezekiel (cf. 13:5), and Third Isaiah (62:1).

Sermon Possibilities

1. Faith's Insight

Those who live by faith in daily communion with God are often able truly to assess situations and persons, when those of no faith cannot do so. John 2:25 tells us that Jesus "knew what was in man," i.e., he could discern character, and Paul writes that when we are new creatures in Christ, we no longer regard anyone from a human point of view (2 Cor. 5:16) — new insight and understanding are given. Our minds are transformed (Rom. 12:2). The outward show and trappings of pretense, material well-being, status, race, gender, performance are bypassed, and we are enabled to see to the heart and to the character, assessing all by its conformity to the will of God. Similarly, when all around us despair and some situation looks hopeless, faith enables us to see events in the light of what God is doing and planning for the future (cf. Jer. 32 or 2 Cor. 4:8-12).

Thus, in this passage from Amos, the prophet sees the true character of Israel. The people of Israel have thought themselves secure, their life guaranteed by their lavish cult (Amos 5:21-24), their wealth (6:1-7), and their military might (6:8-14). Amos on the other hand knows that they are "small," weak and helpless little sinful people with no security in themselves, who cannot possibly stand before the judgment of God (7:2, 5). Perhaps that is the insight of faith that all of us need to see — that our salvation depends solely on Jesus Christ.

2. The Efficacy of Prayer

In fulfillment of his prophetic office, Amos intercedes in this passage for his sinful people, pleading that God will turn aside his judgment from them. And the text tells us that God accedes twice to Amos's prayer. He withholds his judging action and does not bring it upon the people (although later that judgment becomes inevitable, 7:8-9). The point is that intercession is effective. God hears the pleading prayer and acts accordingly. We ought always to pray and not to lose heart, Jesus taught (Luke 18:1).

To be sure, God will answer our prayers according to what is best for us. But Israel was repeatedly saved from destruction by the prayers of its prophets. And how many individuals and churches and even nations have been rescued in past and present by the intercessions of the faithful! Indeed, I sometimes think our children gain more from our prayers before God on their behalf than from all the techniques of child-rearing put together.

3. History's Dialogue

History is one great dialogue between human beings and God, and this passage from Amos illustrates just two little moments in that dialogue. God has uttered his words and done his deeds in history; human beings hear or refuse to hear, and see or refuse to see (cf. Isa. 6:10; 42:19-20; Ezek. 2:7). God then responds in wrath or in love, in judgment or in forgiveness, in grief or in joy. We do not live in a deterministic world; the future is not set forever. It portends good or evil, changes, is altered, by that constant interaction of God and human beings.

To be sure, the end of history is certain. God will bring in his kingdom, and every knee will bow and every tongue confess that Jesus Christ is Lord, to the glory of God the Father (Phil. 2:10-11). But what will happen in the meantime, and whether we will participate in that good and future realm, depends on how we carry on this dialogue of word and deed with our God. God speaks. We respond. God acts accordingly. The Bible is full of accounts of that interaction — that great dialogue with our Lord in which we all are always engaged.

AMOS 8:11-14

Amos 8:1-12 is listed in the three-year lectionary as the stated Old Testament reading for Pentecost 16C. Thus, two verses of that reading, vv. 11-12, are found in our passage.

Actually Amos 8:11-14 is part of the larger section of Amos 8:4–9:6, which can be divided into the separate oracles of 8:4-8, 9-10, 11-14, and 9:1-4, 5-6. The whole section concerns the "end" that is coming upon Israel — the end of her injustice (8:4-8), the end of joy (8:9-10), the end of God's word (8:11-14), the end of her life (9:1-4), and the God of the end (9:5-6).

Features to Note in the Text

V. 11. "The days are coming" signifies an indeterminate time in the future, when Israel realizes that the Day of the Lord is coming upon her (cf. 5:18-20; 8:9) and that her end is near.

V. 12. The picture is one in which the Israelites stagger and run frantically the whole length and breadth of their land, searching for some Word from the Lord.

V. 13. "Thirst" in this verse refers still to thirst for the Word of the Lord (cf. v. 11).

V. 14. Ashimah is the name of an unknown god (cf. 2 Kings 17:13) that was apparently worshiped at the royal sanctuary in Bethel. It was at Bethel and Dan that Jeroboam I erected two golden calves, whose worship replaced that of Yahweh (1 Kings 12:28-29). Beersheba was a place of pilgrimage (cf. Amos 5:5). Israel swears, that is she puts her trust, in these alien gods to secure her life.

Sermon Possibility

1. The Famine of the Word

There are two ways we can experience the famine of the Word of God. First, we ourselves can reject the Word, and the examples of that rejection in our time are legion. It is now possible on the campuses of American colleges and universities to discuss and even tout every religious belief except that of the Christian church. The absolute claims of our faith are taboo in our postmodern world, and relativism is the order of the day. There is no Truth as such. Religions, including the Christian religion, are simply human constructs, each appropriate to its own setting, and no one of them can claim to embody universal and absolute truth. Thus, Christ's claim to be the way, the truth, and the life, and his statement that no one comes to the Father but by him (John 14:6) are rejected out of hand.

Similarly, the belief that the Scriptures mediate the Word of God and consequently form the one authority for faith and practice is now a belief rejected by large numbers of church members in the mainline denominations. In addition, the life of the church is rarely a subject for reports in all forms of the public media. The Word of God, written, preached, or put into practice is not a subject of concern in our society. Our age has rejected it.

Such rejection could be summed up in the story of the crucifixion of Christ. In that event, humankind took the Word of God made flesh and attempted to do away with him forever. We tried to create our own famine of the word.

But in this passage from Amos, the Lord declares that because Israel and we have rejected his word, he himself will withdraw it from us. And we should understand that to mean that God withdraws not only his speaking but also his acting — for God's Word and God's act are one in biblical thought. Consequently, when we get into trouble and go searching frantically about for some word of guidance, some reassurance for the future, some protection lent to us, we will find none of those. God will have withdrawn his word and turned us over to our fate. In Romans, Paul says that God punishes sin by loosing us from his grasp, giving us up, and allowing us to do what we want (Rom. 1:24, 26, 28). In this passage in Amos, God does the same.

We, however, cannot live without the Word of God. It was by his word that God created all things and persons (Gen. 1; John 1:3), and it is by God's Word that all are sustained. We do not live by bread alone, Jesus teaches, but by every word that proceeds from the mouth of God (Matt. 4:4 = Deut. 8:3; cf. John 4:34), and without that word, we will die, as Israel is told she will die, in v. 14 of our passage.

Once again that thought can be enlarged by the cross of Jesus Christ. If the death of the incarnate Word of God on the cross is final, there is not and there cannot be any eternal life. In the word, and by the word, there is life. If there be a famine of the word, there can be only death. Such is the warning of Amos for our faithless generation.

Preaching from the Book of Obadiah

Recommended Commentaries

Elizabeth Achtemeier. *Minor Prophets I.* New International Biblical Commentary. Peabody, Mass.: Hendrickson Publishers, 1996.
James Muilenburg. "Obadiah, Book of." *The Interpreter's Dictionary of the Bible,* vol. 3. New York, Nashville: Abingdon Press, 1962.
John A. Thompson. "The Book of Obadiah. Introduction and Exegesis." *The Interpreter's Bible,* vol. 6. New York, Nashville: Abingdon Press, 1956.

The Historical Context

The prophecy of Obadiah was delivered sometime between 587 and 538 B.C., during the exile of Judah in Babylonia. It is directed against the nation of Edom, that lay to the south-southeast of the southern tip of the Dead Sea. During the reigns of David and Solomon, Israel controlled Edom, but thereafter Edom's territory was frequently the object of wars for its possession, because the main trade route to the Gulf of Aqabah ran through it.

The forbear of the Edomites was Esau, the brother of Jacob (Gen. 25:29-34). From the first their relationship was marked by deceit and hatred (Gen. chs. 27, 32, 33), and their enmity continued among their descendants.

In 587 B.C., when Judah and Jerusalem fell to the armies of the Babylonian Empire, the Edomites joined in the betrayal and pillaging of Judah. They gloated over Judah's downfall (vv. 12-13), looted Jerusalem, entered into the gambling for booty and slaves (v. 11), and captured fleeing Judean refugees and sold them into slavery (v. 14).

The Theological Context

Obadiah's words were given to him in an ecstatic vision (v. 1), and there is contained within them a richness of theological themes. Verses 10-14 concern the obligations inherent in brotherhood and human relations. Verses 3-4, 8 deal with the sinful pride of nations. Verses 15-16, 21 set forth God's lordship over all nations that is to be finally manifested in the Day of the Lord. Verse 15 deals with the consequences of human sin. And vv. 17, 21 take up the theme of a remnant.

Thus, this small book, which at first reading appears so nationalistic and vengeful, is rather a deposit of some of the basic theology of the Scriptures.

OBADIAH 1-4, 10-14, 15-17, 21

Features to Note in the Text

Obadiah is a book of contrasts. If we lay out a table of such contrasts, it looks like this:

> Edom sets itself on high, vv. 3-4.
>> God will bring Edom down, v. 4.
> Edom violates the covenant with Judah, vv. 10-12.
>> The allies of Edom overcome him, v. 7.
> Edom devastates Judah in the day of calamity, vv. 11-13.
>> The Lord has a Day, vv. 8, 15.
> Edom cannot understand, v. 7.
>> The Lord will destroy understanding, v. 8.
> The mount of Esau, vv. 8-9, 19.
>> The mount of Zion, vv. 17, 21.
> Jacob's wealth carried off, vv. 11, 13.
>> Esau's wealth lost, v. 6.

Jacob's restored, v. 17.
Judah's remnant cut off and delivered over, v. 14.
No remnant for Esau, v. 18.
Judah's remnant restored, v. 17.

Sermon Possibilities

1. God's Guard over Human Relationships

Throughout the Scriptures, the many different relationships between human beings concern not just the persons involved, but God. The basic laws given to the people of God in both Old and New Testaments set forth God's concern with relations to parents and spouses and neighbors (Exod. 20:12-17 and parallels). Marriage is guarded (Mal. 2:13-16; Matt. 19:4-6), as are relations with friends and strangers and even enemies (throughout the teachings of Jesus).

Thus, here in Obadiah, Edom is to be judged for its betrayal of its brotherly relation with Judah. The law of Deuteronomy 23:7 forbids Israel from abhorring an Edomite, because "he is your brother." But when Jerusalem was captured, Edom had abhorred Judah and contributed to Judah's devastation and enslavement. Edom therefore was itself to be destroyed in the Day of the Lord, when God would bring his final judgment upon all nations.

God takes human relationships seriously, between husband and wife, brother and sister, friends and neighbors, classes and races, societies and nations. There is no heedless escape into some spiritual realm in the biblical faith, no other-worldly indifference to daily life in our town. No. What we do in our contacts with others is marked and measured by our Lord, and we are responsible for justice and mercy and love toward those whom God has brought into our life. As God has acted toward us, we are to act toward others (cf. 1 John 4:19; cf. Deut. 24:17-22). That is our responsibility before our Lord.

2. Sin Returned

Obadiah shares with other scriptural passages a concept of God's judgment on sinful behavior that links the sinful deed with its punishment. That is, what the sinner does is allowed to return upon his own head (cf. 1 Kings 8:32; Rom. 1:24, 26, 28). Obadiah 15 sets it out clearly for Edom: "As you have done, it shall be done to you,/your deeds shall return on your own head."

The Scriptures do not consider that such judgment is automatic, however, and that we just naturally suffer the consequences of what we have done, in some cause-effect relationship. Rather, our evil deeds return upon our heads because God lets them return (note God's action in 1 Kings 8:32). God looses us from his protecting hand and allows us to be the victims of our sinfulness, as in the Romans passages cited above. Sometimes, of course, in his incredible mercy, God protects us from the results of our folly. Indeed, how often has he so protected us in our daily round! But when our sin is grievous, as is the sin of Edom, God works his destroying judgment, either now or in the future.

3. The Downfall of Pride

Edom is to be judged, according to Obadiah, not only for its rapacity against its brother Judah, but also for its pride. In the pride of its heart, it thought itself absolutely secure, living as it did in a land of natural fortifications. Edom's cliffs rose in three great steps to five thousand feet, and its landscape of mountains, cliffs, rocky defiles, and stony plateaus defied any invader. Thus, Edom boasted, "Who will bring me down to the ground?" (v. 3).

Her boast was like that of so many nations (cf. Isa. 14:12-14). Nazi Germany thought it would enjoy a thousand-year Reich. Great Britain claimed, "There will always be an England, and its colonies beyond the seas." But nations — including ours — forget that there is one Ruler, whose name is Adonai Yahweh (v. 1), Lord God, and that his is the ultimate kingdom (v. 21). Thus no state can claim to be absolute, and no nation can boast either that it is a perfect nation or that its ways accord fully with the will of God. All human governments are provisional, because God's ultimate government — his kingdom — has not yet come on earth in its fullness.

Certainly, in the Scriptures governments are ordained by God to maintain a goodly order and to put down evil-doers (cf. Rom. 13:1-7). But when the government itself becomes evil, rewarding evil and persecuting and punishing good, and when it claims for itself absolute power and security, then it is ripe, as Edom was ripe, for destruction by the Lord of all nations who can pluck up and break down, destroy and overthrow (Jer. 1:10). The nations to God are like "a drop from a bucket," proclaims Second Isaiah (Isa. 40:15), and the Lord can bring princes to nought and make the rulers of the earth as nothing (Isa. 40:23). So Edom will fall, declares Obadiah, with no survivor left to it, at the hand of the Lord God who is the omnipotent Ruler of human history.

On the Lord's Day of final judgment, then, when those who have defied the Lord have been destroyed (Ob. 16), the "saved" (which is the proper reading in Ob. 21) will inherit the earth (cf. "Blessed are the meek, for they shall inherit the earth," Matt. 5:5). And the world of nations will have become the kingdom of our Lord and of his Christ (Rev. 11:15; Ob. 21).

Preaching from the Book of Jonah

Recommended Commentaries

Elizabeth Achtemeier. *Minor Prophets I.* New International Biblical
Commentary. Peabody, Mass.: Hendrickson Publishers, 1996.
Terence E. Fretheim. *The Message of Jonah. A Theological Commentary.*
Minneapolis: Augsburg Publishing House, 1977.

The Historical Context

Jonah is never called a prophet in his book, but he is named as "the son
of Amittai" (1:1). That serves to identify him with the prophet in 2 Kings
14:25, who prophesied during the reign of Jeroboam II (787/6-747/6
B.C.) in Israel.

However, the book of Jonah calls Nineveh a "great city" (1:2), and
we know that Nineveh had little area and importance during the reign
of Jeroboam. It began to grow after 745 B.C. and was finally named the
capital of Assyria by Sennacherib (705-681 B.C.), becoming the most
powerful city in the ancient Near East. It was ultimately reduced to ruins
by the Medes and Babylonians in 612 B.C. and was never restored. The
book of Jonah therefore is looking back on a time when Nineveh was
"great."

It is also looking back on the policy begun under the reign of
Tiglath-pileser III (745-727 B.C.), when Assyria systematically deported
captive peoples and replaced them with an alien population — a policy
that caused Assyria to be universally hated and that enabled Nahum to

term Nineveh a "city of blood" that practiced "endless cruelty" (Nah. 3:1).

It is against such an eighth-century-B.C. background that Jonah is to be understood. However, the book should probably be dated between 500 and 450 B.C. It mirrors precisely the attitude of the time that is found in Malachi 3:14: "It is futile to serve God" (cf. Jonah 4:3). The unknown author of Jonah is telling a didactic story, using eighth-century-B.C. Assyria as the story's setting.

The Theological Context

Above all else, Jonah is a story showing forth the unbounded mercy of the Creator God, who is the Lord and Source of all life, natural and human. The story is not intended to emphasize the miracle of the big fish or to discuss Jonah's reluctance to be shown to be a false prophet. And it is not a protest against the exclusivism of Judaism in the time of Nehemiah and Ezra.

Rather, Jonah portrays the nature of God who is the Creator of all things — of the storm, the fish, the plant, the worm, the scorching east wind, the animals in Nineveh — and who is the Creator of Jonah and the sailors and the Ninevites. All of these are absolutely dependent on God for their existence, as Jonah and the sailors and the Ninevites come to recognize.

This Creator God, however, is totally free (1:14; 3:9; 4:11). He can grant mercy and life to whom he will — to disobedient Jonah and even to wicked Nineveh. God is not coerced by goodness or obedience, by repentance or piety, or even by evil and disobedience. In overwhelming mercy he wills to save. God will not give up even Nineveh, that "city of blood," any more than he will give up Jonah, that self-willed, sulking, angry prophet. In many ways, Jonah is a humorous tale. But it is also an almost incredible presentation of the mercy and love of God, which finally finds its incarnation in our Lord Jesus Christ.

JONAH 1:1-16

Features to Note in the Text

Vv. 2-3. The verb for "arise" in v. 2 is repeated in v. 3. God commands Jonah to "arise," and Jonah "arose." His response is immediate. However, instead of going to Nineveh, he flees in exactly the opposite direction to Tarshish, a name that is repeated three times for emphasis.

The exact location of Tarshish is unknown, but it has most frequently been identified with Tartessus, a Phoenician colony on the southwestern coast of Spain. In the Scriptures it is mentioned as a distant place (Ps. 72:10; Isa. 66:19). Jonah's distancing himself from God is being emphasized.

That distancing is also emphasized by the author's use of spatial terms. Jonah goes down to Joppa (v. 3), he goes down on the ship (v. 3 Hebrew), he goes down into the hold of the ship (v. 5), just as in chapter 2, he goes down toward Sheol, the place of the dead (2:6). To separate oneself from God is to go down to death.

Similarly, that Jonah flees from "the presence of the Lord" is repeated in vv. 2-3, to emphasize that separation.

Jonah is by no means an irreligious man, however. His confession of faith in 1:9 is a standard creedal statement, as is his recitation of one of Israel's oldest creeds in 4:2. Similarly, his thanksgiving song in 2:2-9 is traditional Israelite praise. Jonah is a believer, but he is a fleeing believer who simply does not like the task to which he has been called. Disobedience always has its consequences, however, not only for the believer, but for all those around him, as the book illustrates.

There is no doubt in this chapter as to who is truly God. The sailors' gods cannot still the storm, and when they learn that Jonah worships "the Lord, the God of heaven, who made the sea and dry land" (v. 9), the sailors fearfully realize that they are dealing with the Creator of the universe who can do with them as he pleases. Their conversion in v. 16 comes as the result of the mercy of that Creator.

Sermon Possibility

This chapter obviously contains a multitude of preaching possibilities, as the above features suggest. However, I will deal with only one.

1. Escaping God

Jonah's intent is to "flee to Tarshish from the presence of the Lord" (v. 3) — in short, to get away from God. The question is, Is that possible? Is it possible to go to some place where God is not?

Obviously, other writers of the Scriptures do not think so. Job would have loved to escape God's presence just long enough to swallow his spittle, and he could not do so (Job 7:19). "If I ascend to heaven," testified the Psalmist, "thou art there. If I make my bed in Sheol, thou art there!" (Ps. 139:8), a thought repeated in fearful terms in Amos 9:2-3. At the end of his ministry, our Lord told his disciples, "Lo, I am with you always to the close of the age" (Matt. 28:20), a promise always considered by us to be gracious, though perhaps we have never thought through all that it entails.

Jonah would gladly have escaped from God, but he probably knew he could not do so. He knew very well who was causing the great wind and mighty tempest that threatened the sailors' ship. He knew who summoned the fish and the plant, the worm and the hot east wind, and the sun to cause him discomfort. Behind all the unhappy happenings of his mission, he saw the ever-present person of the Lord. Nevertheless, his initial attempt was to escape from God's presence. Is that possible?

In one sense, it is. Jonah was going to a pagan place named Tarshish, far away from that promised land where a Jewish community of faith worshiped and cherished the Scripture and practiced the Torah. Jonah was going to Tarshish where the name of Yahweh was not spoken and where other gods or no gods were the objects of commitment and where life was lived as if there were no Lord of heaven and earth.

So too can we flee to our own Tarshish. We can so immerse ourselves in our irreligious society or in a godless social circle or in our own affairs and interests that the name of God is never spoken except in profanity and the works of God are never recalled. We can absent ourselves from all worship, all faith communities, all religious learning, all attempts to live by faith's ethic, and become totally secular — banishing God from our thought, our deeds, our devotion, our total view of the world. We can forget about God and live in "Tarshish." And perhaps Tarshish is a good name for our present culture.

God, of course, is not absent from such a culture. God, who sustains each life and the order of the natural realm, is never absent.

But we can forget him and his word and works, and live as if he does not exist, as Jonah wanted to do.

When the Scriptures talk about sin, they often talk about forgetting. When Psalms 78 and 106 recount the history of Israel's sin, they do so by saying that Israel "forgot" what God had done (Ps. 78:11), or she "did not remember" the abundance of God's steadfast love (Ps. 106:7), or she "forgot his works" (Ps. 106:13), or "they forgot God, their Savior" (Ps. 106:21). They lived in the forgetfulness of "Tarshish."

Thus, Jesus can ask his disciples, "Do you not remember?" (Mark 8:18), and the angel at the empty tomb can tell the women, "Remember how he told you . . ." (Luke 24:6). "Remember the word that I said to you," Jesus admonishes (John 15:20), and the author of 2 Timothy commands, "Remember Jesus Christ, risen from the dead" (2:8). In short, live not in the amnesia of Tarshish, but in the communal remembrance that is given to you through pulpit and song, Scripture and prayer, sacrament and Christian practice. Take up your spiritual residence where the name of God is known and spoken, adored and obeyed. For as with Jonah, to flee from God is go down to death. To obey and love him is life, and his wondrous mercy always.

JONAH CHAPTERS 3 AND 4

Jonah 3:1-5, 10 is the stated lesson in the three-year lectionary for Epiphany 3B. It is paired with Mark 1:14-20, whose call is for repentance and discipleship; with 1 Corinthians 7:29-31, that deals with the coming End before which all should repent; and with Psalm 62:5-12, that affirms that in God alone are refuge, power, and salvation.

Features to Note in the Text

3:2-3. The first words of v. 2 repeat God's initial command in 1:2. This time Jonah obeys.

3:4. Jonah preaches after going only one day into the city. The power of the Word of God is being emphasized.

3:5-8. The news of Jonah's proclamation spreads among the people, who immediately enter into a fast of repentance. When the news reaches the king, the fast is extended even to the animals. The implication is that nature too is fallen and needs to repent and be redeemed. Further, the king asks from the people a transformation of character that eschews violence.

3:9. The king of Nineveh knows that their repentance will not automatically turn aside God's judgment. Rather, God must "have compassion," that is, exercise his free mercy.

4:2. The reason for Jonah's flight is revealed. He tried to flee from God, because he knew God would forgive Nineveh, and Jonah did not want God to forgive them.

4:2. The description of God is a standard creedal form, found throughout the Old Testament (Exod. 34:6-7; 2 Chron. 30:9; Neh. 9:17; Ps. 86:15; 103:8; 111:4; Joel 2:13, et al.).

4:5. Jonah stations himself outside of the city to see if God will change his mind and destroy Nineveh.

4:6. Jonah already has shade from the booth, v. 5. The shade of the plant, therefore, is probably a symbol of God's gracious protection. (Cf. the use of the symbol in Ps. 121:5; Isa. 4:6; 25:4.)

4:8. The sultry east wind is the sirocco that blows in off of the desert, wilting everything before it.

Sermon Possibilities

As with chapter 1, these two chapters are rich with content that could be used in several sermons. However, I will suggest only three possibilities.

1. Slow to Anger

Jonah confesses in the traditional words of 4:2 that God is "slow to anger," and the whole story confirms that characterization. At the beginning of chapter 3, God does not give Jonah the rebuke he deserves for his previous disobedience and attempt at flight. He gives him another chance. God does not immediately bring his judgment upon wicked Nineveh, but gives them forty days to repent of their evil. And in chapter 4, Jonah's anger at God (vv. 1, 9) and his blatant blasphemy in v. 9 bring only the mildest questions from the Lord of the universe. This is the God who is very slow to anger.

For years God lets us pursue our evil doings. Like a patient Father, he allows us our childish freedom and rebellions, rebuking us only occasionally with the consequences of our actions. Then when his sentence of judgment is brought home to us through the Holy Spirit that illumines his Word, he still delays in bringing disaster and death upon us, always giving us time to turn, always repeating his wooing words of love, always urging us by church and conscience, or by faithful friend and illumining circumstance to repent and return to him. God's is an incredible patience and mercy that wills our life and not our death. The God of Jonah and of all the Scriptures is very slow to anger.

2. Jonah the Judge

Throughout his story, Jonah sets himself up as the judge of God. He thinks he knows very well what God should do and how the affairs of the world should be handled. God commands Jonah to preach to Nineveh, but Jonah thinks that such an evil city should not even hear the Word of God. And above all, Jonah believes that such a "city of blood" should not be forgiven. By his actions, Jonah criticizes God and judges the Lord's will to be wrong.

Thus when Jonah displays his anger at God in 4:1-2, he then goes out to the east of the city and sits down to see if maybe God has gotten the point of his criticism and will destroy Nineveh after all (4:5). Surely God will realize his mistake, accept Jonah's assessment of the situation, and bring destruction on the evil Assyrians. After all, evil people should get what they deserve. Jonah knows that, and he hopes that God will learn the lesson from him.

When God does not let himself be instructed by his proud and angry prophet, when God instead exhibits his sovereignty by the little means of a castor oil plant, a worm, and a sirocco, Jonah wants to die (4:9), just as Jonah earlier expressed that desire because Nineveh was not immediately destroyed (4:3). God is incorrigible; he won't learn a thing (cf. Isa. 40:13-14). He can't get it through his head that evil should be punished, and so there is no structure of justice in the world, and Jonah just wants to be quit of the whole business. If the wicked do not get their just reward, then there is no sense to God and faith, and a person might as well end it all. The life of faith is meaningless. Death is to be preferred (cf. Mal. 2:17).

How often we modern-day Jonahs are sure that God should punish some person, that their sin has placed them outside of the realm of grace, and that they should never be forgiven — not by us, not by anyone, and certainly not by God.

Or how often we come to believe that there is no justice in the world, that the good we do should be rewarded (but see Luke 17:10), while the wicked should be punished. And when that does not happen, we cynically decide that "life is unfair" and become despairing Jonahs, while all the time God continues gently to teach us, as he did with his despairing prophet. When we try to subject God to our rules, nothing makes sense. When instead we submit our lives to his good leading, then we are given meaning and purpose.

3. Sovereign Grace

God is constantly on the scene in the book of Jonah, hurling the storm, appointing and speaking to the fish, repenting of evil, appointing the plant and worm and wind. And each one of those verbs in this book sets forth actions of a sovereign Lord of all creation. But they also manifest the actions of a sovereign Lord of grace.

God continually deals graciously with Jonah, despite Jonah's disobedience. There is no reason why Jonah should have been saved by a great fish and then deposited safely on dry land, no reason why he should have been preserved to be given his mission a second time, no reason why he should even have a castor oil plant to shade his head from the desert sun. And given all of those acts of grace, large and small, Jonah never does repent of his disobedience. Nevertheless, God lets him experience what grace is like.

But God also lets Jonah experience judgment, both great and small — peril in the belly of the fish and the threat of death, followed by discomfort and faintness in the heat — just little judgments that could not be compared to what Nineveh would experience.

From both of those — grace and judgments, big and small — God wants Jonah to learn. He wants Jonah to learn that his life is totally in the hands of God. But he also wants Jonah to realize that, above all else, the Sovereign over life is very gracious. God wants life and good, not only for all of us disobedient Jonahs, but for the Ninevites of the world — for the Judases and Hitlers, the Pol Pots and the Stalins, the Maos and the Moons and every terrorist. God wants life for those who hung his Son on a cross and for those thieves who died beside him. God wants good for the most grievous sinner and for the most ignorant, good for children and cattle (Jon. 4:11) and all of the creatures on the face of his earth. It is almost impossible for us to comprehend the "breadth and length and height and depth" of God's love for his world in Jesus Christ. That love "surpasses knowledge" (Eph. 3:18-19). But perhaps the charming little story of Jonah can aid us toward that comprehension.

Preaching from the Book of Micah

Recommended Commentaries

Elizabeth Achtemeier. *Minor Prophets I.* New International Biblical
    Commentary. Peabody, Mass: Hendrickson Publishers, 1996.
Delbert R. Hillers. *Micah.* Hermeneia. Philadelphia: Fortress Press,
    1984.
James Luther Mays. *Micah.* The Old Testament Library. Philadelphia:
    The Westminster Press, 1976.

The Historical Context

Although the superscription to Micah states that he prophesied during
the reigns of the Judean kings Jotham (742-735 B.C.), Ahaz (735-715
B.C.), and Hezekiah (715-687 B.C.), probably the first collection of
oracles in the book dates from about 701 B.C. To this first collection,
additions were continually made, and the final form of the book took
shape after 515 B.C.

Micah's home was in Moresheth, some twenty-five miles southwest
of Jerusalem, but his preaching was probably carried on in the capital
city amidst a very turbulent time in Judah's history.

The mighty empire of Assyria held sway over the smaller states of
the Near East. Micah anticipates both the fall of the northern kingdom
of Israel to Sargon II in 721 B.C. (Mic. 1:6-7) and the destruction of
Judah and Jerusalem by the armies of Sennacherib in 701 B.C. (1:10-16;
2:4-5; 3:12). Both defeats brought deportations of large sections of the

Hebrew populations. Indeed, the inhabitants of the northern kingdom were swallowed up forever. Judah lost forty-six of her surrounding cities and Jerusalem was saved only by Hezekiah's payment of a large tribute to Assyria (2 Kings 18:13-16). It is against this background that Micah's message alternates between oracles of judgment and of salvation.

The Theological Context

Although chapters 4–7 have often been denied to Micah himself, the book must be understood as a whole. It represents over two centuries of Israel's meditations on her God-given role in the world of nations. (Note that the book begins and ends with the nations, 1:2 and 7:16.) All are set against the background of God's promise to the patriarchs to bring blessing on all the families of the earth through Israel (Gen. 12:3b; cf. Mic. 7:20).

The question behind the book is, How can God use Israel as the medium of his blessing on all nations when Israel is sinful? Judah is shot through with oppression of the poor (2:1-3, 9), corrupt courts and judges (3:1-3, 11), dishonest commercial practices (6:10-11), false prophecy (3:5-7), greedy priests (3:11), loss of communal order (7:2-6), and abhorrence of God's justice and commandments (3:9-12). How can such a nation be the instrument of God?

The answer is that God will first judge Israel, giving her up to Assyria. But then he will save a remnant of the people (2:12-13; 4:6-7, 8, 10, 11-13; 7:8-10, 11-13, 18-20) and will give them a future Davidic king (Messiah) to rule over them (5:2-4).

When other nations see God's salvation of Israel, some of them will be led to repent and to turn to the Lord (7:10, 15-17). Those who do not and who continue to oppose Israel will be destroyed (4:11-13; 5:5-6, 8-9, 10-15), in fulfillment of the promise of Genesis 12:3a. Those remaining will then inherit, along with Israel's remnant, a realm of peace in the kingdom of God (4:1-4; 5:2-5, 7).

MICAH 3:9-12

Features to Note in the Text

This passage is a summary of the indictments that Micah has leveled against Jerusalem's leaders in the preceding oracles. It forms the climactic announcement of the destruction of Jerusalem.

The Hebrew of v. 9 proclaims that those with authority in Judah "abhor *mišpaṭ*" and "pervert uprightness." *Mišpaṭ* or "justice" here refers in the widest sense to God's order for the covenant community. That order was set forth in God's Torah, and was the guide by which Judah was to direct her life. It was to be taught by prophets and priests, and it included not only God's commandments, but the whole of the sacred tradition, encompassing all of God's words and deeds for Israel in the past and present.

V. 10 may be a reference to Hezekiah's employment of forced labor for his extensive building projects.

V. 11 refers to bribes given to judges to influence their legal decisions, to priests who will teach the Torah only when they are paid to do so, and to prophets who pronounce words of comfort and weal for those who give them large sums of money.

The reference of v. 11 to the Lord's dwelling in the midst of the people is to the presence of the ark of the covenant in the Holy of Holies, the inner room of the temple. The ark was a rectangular box, with a gold slab called the "mercy seat" on its top. At each end of the mercy seat was a cherub with outspread wings. And above the cherubim's wings, the Lord was invisibly enthroned (cf. 2 Sam. 4:4). Thus where the ark was, God was present.

Sermon Possibilities

1. The Result of Conformity

"Do not be conformed to this world," Paul writes (Rom. 12:2). Everywhere the Scriptures warn against conducting our lives according to the standards and customs of the society in which we live. The Israelites were instructed by God not to "do as they do in the land of Egypt, where you dwelt," and not to "do as they do in the land of Canaan, to which I am bringing you" (Levit. 18:3). Indeed, Jesus' teaching in the Sermon on the Mount (Matt. chs. 5–7) literally turned the ways of this world upside down and urged upon us a righteousness unknown in human affairs — the forgiveness of enemies, the ways of meekness and mercy, sole reliance upon God for the goods of life.

But if we are not to conform to the society in which we live, from where do we get our directions for life? This and many other passages in the Scriptures make the answer clear — from God, from God's *mišpat*, God's justice, God's ordering Torah.

There is recounted for us in the Bible a tradition spanning some two thousand years of history, in which we find an entirely unique worldview — a view that sees all of life related to God, that recounts his deeds of love and mercy and forgiveness over and over again and commands us to imitate them, that holds that life cannot be lived in joy and security except it is lived in relationship to the Lord. And within that history there are words, commandments, teachings, stories, that constantly point the way to abundant life. "Torah" in the Bible has the basic meaning of "teaching," of "pointing the finger": "This is the way; walk in it!"

We learn that way by immersing ourselves in the story, by reading and studying time and again of what God has said and done. We absorb the story into our hearts, until we know it by memory and automatically follow its ways. Then we are, as Paul writes in Romans, "transformed by the renewal of our minds," and we become able to do the will of God, which is good and acceptable and perfect (Rom. 12:2).

But apart from that transformation, apart from living into the story and getting it into our bones, we become like the leaders and judges, the priests and prophets in our Micah passage — abhorers of God's *mišpat*, perverters of his Torah, selfishly seeking our own ends and building our society with blood.

The catch is that the Scriptures' worldview, though we have rejected it, is actually the only reality. All of life is responsible to God and directed by him, and when we defy his *mišpat* for our lives, he will bring judgment upon us (Mic. 3:12). Jerusalem, as in Micah's prophecy, became in fact a "heap of ruins," as every life and every society will know ruin apart from God.

2. "God Be With You"?

"Lo, I am with you always, to the close of the age" (Matt. 28:20). Thus did our Lord reassure his disciples before he left them to ascend into heaven. And we have always taken that as a very comforting thought.

Like the Judeans in the time of Micah, we have confirmed, "Is not the Lord in the midst of us? No evil shall come upon us" (Mic. 3:11).

The Judeans rested their confidence on the fact that the Lord was invisibly enthroned above the ark of the covenant in the temple, dwelling in the midst of his people in the darkness of the Holy of Holies. We rest our confidence on Jesus' presence with us. And so we have our popular phrases, "God be with you," or "Go with God." We even put it in a popular song in the past, "Vaya con Dios." If God or Jesus is with us, "no evil shall come upon us."

We can be very blasé about it, and the Judeans could be very blasé, failing to realize who God is. But the prophet Micah knew very well.

> Behold, the Lord is coming forth out of his place,
>   and will come down and tread upon the high places of the earth.
> And the mountains will melt under him,
>   and the valleys will be cleft,
> like wax before the fire,
>   like waters poured down a steep place. (1:3-4)

Micah knew very well that the Lord of heaven and earth could be a consuming fire before whose presence the very mountains would melt; that God descended to earth in smoke and fire accompanied by trumpet blast and shaking earth (Exod. 19:18-19; Judg. 5:4-5); that no human being could see God and live (Deut. 5:25-26). He could very well agree with Amos Wilder's portrayal of worshiping such a God:

> Going to church is like approaching an open volcano
> where the world is molten
> and hearts are sifted.
> The altar is like a third rail that spatters sparks,
> the sanctuary is like the chamber next the atomic oven:
> there are invisible rays and you leave your watch outside.[1]

Micah also knew that such a God could not put up with sin (cf. Hab. 1:13) and that therefore he was coming to destroy the people of Israel because of their sin:

---

1. "Electric Chimes or Rams' Horns," *Grace Confounding* (Philadelphia: Fortress Press, 1972), p. 13.

All this is for the transgression of Jacob
and for the sins of the house of Israel. (Mic. 1:5)

Thus, we worshipers of the Lord need to ask ourselves, In what manner is the Lord always with us: in wrath and judgment or love and mercy? Do we in his holy presence expect him to protect us from final destruction, no matter what we have done? Or do we humbly bow before him in repentance and love, relying totally on his mercy to forgive us our wrong? Do we in fact welcome his purging judgments that he may remake us into new persons in Christ? Or do we glibly assume that he accepts us just as we are, selfish sinners who have abandoned God's order for our lives?

God be with you? Yes, he will always be with us, as our Lord promised. But he may do with us what we never imagined.

MICAH 5:1-4

Micah 5:2-5a is the stated lesson in the three-year lectionary for the fourth Sunday in Advent in Cycle C. As such, it is paired with Psalm 80:1-7, which is a prayer that God, the Shepherd of Israel, will save his people; with Luke 1:39-45 (46-55), the visit of Mary to her cousin Elizabeth that points toward the fulfillment of prophecy; and with Hebrews 10:5-10 that proclaims Christ to be the all-sufficient sacrifice for sin.

Features to Note in the Text

The lectionary has omitted v. 1, but that verse is important for understanding the context. It begins with the word "now" in the Hebrew and is the third in the series of three oracles that open with that word, 4:9-10; 4:11-13; and 5:1-4. All three passages describe Judah's present desperate situation in the present ("now"), but then promise the Lord's future salvation of his people.

That pattern is found here. The first two lines in v. 1 probably refer to the siege of Jerusalem in 588 B.C. The last two lines in that verse refer to the humiliation of the davidic king Jehoiachin, who was taken into Babylonian exile in 597 B.C. Further, v. 3 recalls 4:10 and compares the trek into Babylonian captivity to the travail of a woman in childbirth. (See my commentary on this verse.)

In contrast to Judah's present desperate situation "now," the prophecy promises a future davidic ruler from God — a *mašiah*, an anointed one, a Messiah — whose reign will endure forever ("stand"), who will rule in the strength and majesty given him by God, whose kingdom will be universal, and who will grant to God's people return to their homeland and security forever.

Sermon Possibilities

1. Understanding the "But"

There it is again, that "but," just like the "but" that we find in so many places in the Scriptures: "The grass withers, the flower fades; *but* the word of our God will stand for ever" (Isa. 40:8); "The women who had come with him from Galilee followed, and saw the tomb, and how his body was laid. . . . *But* on the first day of the week, at early dawn, they went to the tomb. . . . *but* when they went in they did not find the body" (Luke 23:55; 24:1, 3).

God keeps taking our present desperate circumstances — all the wrongs that lay siege to our life's security, all the humiliations to which our sin subjects us — and instead of abandoning us to our follies and destruction, he turns the whole future scenario of our lives upside down: "But!" "Nevertheless!" "Despite all!"

And so Judah here — like us — is promised a Deliverer from our sin, as Hebrews has it; a Shepherd as in Psalm 80 who will guide and feed and protect us; a Ruler, a Lord, as in the Gospel, who will order our ways and give us a peace and security that the world can neither give nor ever take away. No "proud" and "mighty" will trample our lives in the kingdom of this Lord (cf. Luke 1:51-52). No, he will rule by God's strength, and God's will alone will be done.

We should have known that such a Ruler would come, because God promised it, and God always keeps his promises. There will never be lacking a davidic heir to sit upon your throne, God had promised King David way back there in the tenth century B.C. (2 Sam. 7:16). "And I will establish the throne of his kingdom for ever. I will be his father, and he shall be my son" (2 Sam. 7:13-14).

So perhaps what we need in the midst of our sin-saturated situation is to remember the promises of God — to search them out in the Scriptures and to believe them and act upon them. That is what faith means in much of the Bible — to rely on the promises of God (cf. Gen. 15:6; Hebr. 11:1). For then, in whatever situation we find ourselves or no matter what outrageous fortune brings upon us, we shall always know that God has a "nevertheless," a "but," and we can live in contentment and joy (cf. Phil. 4:11-13).

2. The Mysteries of God

The apostle Paul tells us in 1 Corinthians 4:1 that we Christians are "stewards of the mysteries of God." And of course stewards are those to whom something is entrusted. For example, a wine steward is one who is given the task of storing the wine, of keeping it from spoilage and corruption, and of serving it at the proper time. So we Christians are those who are entrusted with God's mysteries, who are to keep them from being corrupted in any way, and who are responsible for distributing them to others.

Here in this passage we are given one of God's mysteries. The davidic ruler, the Messiah who is to come in the future in fulfillment of God's promise, will be one whose "origin is from of old, from ancient days" (v. 2; cf. Dan. 7:9, 13, 22). That is, his origin is beyond human comprehension, from the mysterious realm of God, which no human being can fully fathom. Second, his birth was planned long ago (cf. Hab. 3:6), as part of God's eternal plan for his universe.

We must remember this passage when we speak of its fulfillment by our Messiah, Jesus Christ. He is certainly a man, flesh and blood as are we. Verse 2 specifically states that the Messiah shall come "from you," from Judah's lineage. And except our Savior be like one of us, he cannot deal with our sin and death. He must be human to take upon himself and to defeat human evil.

But his origin is also mysteriously from the realm of God. Our Messiah is not merely a man, not just a Galilean peasant or revolutionary, not simply a human hero or model, not just an extraordinary teacher or prophet or wise man. No, he is also one from God, incarnated in the virgin's womb by the Spirit of God (Matt. 1:20; Luke 1:35), descended from the eternal realm of the Trinity (John 3:13) as the Word of God made flesh.

And except that be true, we have not been freed from our captivity to sin and death, for only God, the source of all life and good, has the power to liberate us from the evil with which we have infested his earth. Try as we may by our own efforts and resources, we cannot always do the good and we cannot escape the obliterating death that is the wages of our evil. But God has redeemed us from our slavery by coming to us "from of old, from ancient days" in his Son, Jesus Christ our Lord.

3. Permanence

Nothing lasts in this world of ours. Empires rise and fall. Peoples and cultures disappear. The best achievements, the loftiest dreams, the most cherished relationships are lost in the passage of years. And our scientists — and the Scriptures — tell us that even heaven and earth shall pass away (Isa. 51:6). "All flesh is grass, and all its beauty is like the flower of the field. The grass withers, the flower fades . . ." (Isa. 40:6-7).

But over against the transitory sorrows of our fading lives, this passage proclaims a permanence — a Messiah whose kingdom will endure forever by the power and majesty of everlasting God, a Shepherd whose protection will afford his flock an inviolable security, a Ruler whose sway will extend over all that exists. It is the same message announced by God in Second Isaiah: ". . . the heavens will vanish like smoke, the earth will wear out like a garment . . . but my salvation will be for ever, and my deliverance will never be ended" (Isa. 51:6).

Nothing lasts in this world of ours. But God lasts. And his Messiah lasts. And his kingdom lasts. And by faith we can enter into that permanence.

MICAH 6:1-8

This passage, whose last verse is so often quoted, is the stated lesson for Epiphany 4A in the three-year lectionary. As such, it is paired with Psalm 15 and Matthew 5:1-12, both of which recount the righteous living expected of those who trust and obey God, and with 1 Corinthians 1:18-31, which grounds our righteousness firmly in the righteousness of Jesus Christ.

Features to Note in the Text

The whole passage is a court case between the Lord and his covenant people Israel. The Lord is the plaintiff, Israel is the accused, and the mountains, hills, and foundations of the earth (thought of as pillars that anchored the earth in the subterranean waters) serve as the witnesses or jury, vv. 1-2. The plaintiff, God, presents his accusation first, vv. 3-5, Israel replies in vv. 6-7, and the sentence is implied in v. 8, where the prophet tells what Israel should have done but has not done.

Exceedingly important for understanding the whole passage is the second line of v. 3, which is the indictment God brings against the people. They are "wearied" with the Lord; their patience with him is exhausted (cf. the same meaning of the verb in Isa. 7:13). Israel is in some kind of trouble that is not specified, and she has lost all patience and hope while waiting for the Lord to deliver her.

It is such wearied impatience that continues when an Israelite spokesman replies to God's charge in vv. 6-7. What does it take for God to come to Israel's rescue? is the implied question. Does he want burnt offerings, or calves a year old that are so much more valuable than newborns? Would God be satisfied with thousands of rams, like Solomon offered (1 Kings 8:63), or literal rivers of precious olive oil used for food and healing? Or maybe, the disgusted speaker says, God would prefer child sacrifice that was forbidden in the law (Levit. 18:21; 20:2-5; Deut. 18:10) and condemned by the prophets as a pagan practice (cf. Jer. 7:31 et al.). What does it take to appease an implacable deity? That is Israel's exasperated question.

Israel has forgotten God's saving deeds in the past, God tells her in vv. 4-5 — his redemption of her out of slavery in Egypt; his gift of the law through Moses, of atonement through the priest Aaron, and of guidance through the prophetess Miriam. The people have forgotten God's deliverance of them from the curse of Balak and Balaam, and his guidance of them through the Jordan from Shittim to their first encampment in Gilgal.

Contrary to the Israelite speaker's sarcastic list of what God might require, his prophet enumerates in v. 8 those deeds that God does in fact command of his people — justice *(mišpaṭ)*, covenant love *(ḥeseḏ)*, and attentive *(haṣenē'a)* walking with him.

Mišpaṭ in this context signifies God's order for the whole of life. It includes legal justice, but its meaning is much broader than that. To do justice is to order every area of life in accord with God's will.

Ḥeseḏ is sometimes translated "kindness" or "mercy," but it is a covenant concept, which means to be faithful to one's covenant with God and with one's fellows, to be bound together in solidarity with them, to be a community that lives in steadfast loyalty to God and to other human beings. And Israel is bidden here to "love" such *ḥeseḏ*.

Finally, Israel is told that she is expected to walk "humbly" with her God. But *haṣenē'a* means much more than simply "modestly," "in a lowly manner," or "self-effacingly." It here includes the meaning of "attentively," "paying attention to," "watching." In short, Israel is to pay attention to God's will and not her own, is to watch God for what is good and not make up her own goods, is to be attentive always to her relationship with God and not follow her own ways. And if Israel will do that, she will "love *ḥeseḏ*" and "do *mišpaṭ*". Thus, this final demand makes possible the fulfillment of the other two.

It is these three requirements that Israel has failed to carry out, and so the implication is that she stands guilty in this court case with God.

Sermon Possibilities

The possibilities for preaching from this passage are multitudinous. Sermons could deal separately with each of the requirements listed in v. 8, because all are integral to living a Christian life. Or the preacher might show what place God's commandments have in the gospel. Or a sermon could treat the last judgment and the fact that finally we all will be summoned to court with our God (cf. 2 Cor. 5:10). Even God's final destiny for Israel could be considered (cf. Rom. ch. 11). However, I shall suggest only two preaching possibilities.

1. Our Instructions

We live in an age and in a society that has elevated the autonomous individual to a place of supreme importance. It is the individual's welfare, sensitivities, and choices that must be considered at all cost, and society is to be shaped accordingly. Similarly, it is the autonomous individual alone who can say what is right or wrong for him or her, and no other moral code or authority can be superimposed on the individual's determination.

The Scriptures and this passage in particular, however, know that finally only God can define what is right and good, because God alone is totally good (cf. Mark 10:18). Our morality is always corrupted by our sinfulness that is evidenced in our propensity to rationalize our wrongs and selfishly to favor our own cause and well-being.

God, however, who is pure goodness, defines what is good, and it is good because he says it as Lord over our lives. There is no other standard of good outside of him, and no action or word can be good unless it accords with his good will. As the Heidelberg Catechism says, only those are good works "which are done out of true faith, in accordance with the Law of God, and for his glory, and not those based on our own opinion or on the traditions of men" (Question 91). Justice, righteousness, mercy, peace — all are defined by what God wills and not by what we will or want.

The good news is that God tells us what is good — tells us how to conduct ourselves, informs us throughout the Scriptures how to lead lives that accord with his will. And this passage is part of that information. If we want abundant life, doing *mišpaṭ,* and loving *ḥeseḏ,* and walking attentively with our God, this passage will help lead us toward it, for God's is the way to life. And he instructs us with these words, because he loves us.

2. The Importance of Remembering

So many times in the Scriptures, Israel and we are commanded to "remember."

> "You shall *remember* that you were a slave in the land of Egypt and the Lord your God redeemed you from there." (Deut. 24:18)

And that remembrance of the Lord's mercy becomes the basis of mercy toward others.

> "Remember how he told you, while he was still in Galilee, that the Son of Man must be delivered into the hands of sinful men, and be crucified, and on the third day rise."

And that remembrance helps the women at the tomb realize that their Lord has risen from the dead.

So here in this passage from Micah, Israel is bidden to "remember" God's saving acts toward her in the past (cf. v. 5), both to indict her for her impatient attitude toward God and to change that attitude. "Bless the Lord, O my soul, and forget not all his benefits" (Ps. 103:2).

It is absolutely essential that we remember what God has done for us, both as individuals and as a church or a society or a nation, for several reasons.

First, memory of God's acts on our behalf forms the basis of gratitude. We remember all of the marvelous things God has done. As Psalm 103 has it, he has forgiven us, guided us, showered on us mercy, at times healed us, heaped upon us benefits large and small. And gratitude for all of that lifts us out of our selfish concern for ourselves and leads us to thankful praise. Gratitude is the cure for lots of human ills, from grumpiness to despair. We cannot remain turned inward on our own miseries when we turn outward in thankfulness to God.

Second, memory of God's "saving acts" (v. 5) forms the basis of our hope for the future. The Scriptures' record of God's mighty acts toward his people gives us assurance that he will never desert us and that our future lies secure in his hands. God, throughout the story of Israel, always kept his promises. And on the basis of his faithfulness in the past we know with surety that he will be faithful to his promises to us in the future. He *will* be with us always. He *will* bring that good work that he began in us to its completion in the day of Jesus Christ (Phil. 1:6). He *will* bring in his kingdom on earth, even as it is in heaven. And he *will* give us eternal life in that kingdom. We remember, and so we face the future with confidence.

Finally, remembrance of God's saving deeds in the past gives us patience in the midst of tribulation. We may be suffering, and all around us may seem dark, with no way out of what we are going through. But God acted for us in the past; God has rescued us before; and so we wait patiently for his salvation in his good time. "They who wait for the Lord shall renew their strength, they shall mount up with wings like eagles, they shall run and not be weary, they shall walk and not faint" (Isa. 40:31). Or perhaps the words of Paul, our fellow sufferer, are most pertinent: "I consider that the sufferings of this present time are not worth comparing with the glory that is to be revealed" (Rom. 8:18). God's final salvation comes. We remember that he promised that. And so we wait in patience.

MICAH 7:18-20

Features to Note in the Text

God is incomparable in this passage because he forgives the sins of the remnant of Israel and the sins of the foreign nations: v. 19c reads in the Hebrew, "Thou wilt cast all their sins into the depths of the sea."

The reason for God's forgiveness is given in the last line of v. 18, which begins with *ki*, "for," "because." God forgives in order to show *ḥesed* or faithfulness to his promise to Abraham (v. 20). God had promised Abraham that his descendants would be the medium through which God would bring blessing on all the families of the earth (Gen. 12:3). By forgiving Israel and using her as the instrument of his salvation, God will keep his promise.

Sermon Possibility

1. What Makes God Incomparable?

People worship many different gods these days — Sophia, the Mother Goddess, Allah, Baal, various gurus, the named and unnamed deities of a hundred different sects and movements. Sometimes they even invent a deity, or the object of their worship is themselves. But amidst the multitude of deities, there is one God who is incomparable and therefore finally the only God, and this passage celebrates him.

There are many reasons the God of Israel is incomparable, and throughout, the Scriptures witness to that uniqueness. He is more powerful than any other god, delivering his people from Egypt when the gods of that empire were helpless to prevent the exodus (Exod. 12:12). He holds the whole sweep of history in his hands, telling what is to come and then bringing it to pass (Isa. 41:22-23). He controls the forces of death and can deliver his own from the clutches of the grave (Ps. 16:10). He delivers the weak and poor and helpless from the powers in society that would destroy them (Ps. 146:7-9). But here in this passage God is celebrated as incomparable because he forgives sin.

There is a sense in which it is proper to fear God, because God is not mocked. One of my friends put it rather too crudely, "If you don't do right, God will zap you." However, God does not wink at sin, and we cannot blithely ignore or defy his will without suffering the consequences. God will maintain his lordship over all of our lives, and call us to account for our actions, and bring his just sentence upon us. The wages of sin is death.

Yet God's attitude toward our wrongdoing is manifested not so much in wrath as in grief (cf. Gen. 6:6; Luke 19:41-42), and finally when it comes to giving his people over to destruction and death in retribution for their iniquity, God will not do so (Hos. 11:8-9). He has promised to be our God in his covenant of steadfast love, and he will not let the forces of death wrest us from his grasp (Rom. 8:38-39; 1 Cor. 15:54-56) or cause him to be unfaithful to his promise.

So he sends his only begotten Son to hang on a cross. That Son gasps out that merciful prayer, "Father, forgive them, for they know not what they do" (Luke 23:34), and then dies the death that we deserve for our sins. And finally, on Easter morn, Jesus Christ rises victorious over all evil and sin and wrong. Because of that we can pray in accord with the prayer of Micah, "Thou, O Lord, art incomparable, and there is no God like thee, because thou hast forgiven our sins in faithfulness to your promise to our fathers."

Preaching from the Book of Nahum

Recommended Commentaries

Elizabeth Achtemeier. *Nahum — Malachi.* Interpretation: A Bible Commentary for Teaching and Preaching. Atlanta: John Knox Press, 1986.

John Calvin. *Commentaries on the Twelve Minor Prophets.* Translated by J. Owen. Edinburgh: Printed for the Calvin Translation Society, 1948.

The Historical Context

Internal evidence in the Book of Nahum indicates that it was compiled sometime between 663 B.C., when ancient Thebes was destroyed by Assyria (Nah. 3:8), and 612 B.C., when Nineveh fell to the Babylonians. Probably its oracles were proclaimed shortly before the fall of that capital city of the Assyrian Empire.

That empire of the eighth and seventh centuries B.C. was noted for its cruelty in its conquest of the smaller states of the ancient Near East. Not only did its armies wreak total destruction upon their captives' lands, but they also systematically deported defeated peoples and replaced them with foreign populations. It was at the hands of Assyria, for example, that the ten northern tribes of Israel were led away to exile in 721 B.C., to disappear forever from history.

Nineveh, the capital of Assyria, symbolized that cruelty in the years that followed its rise to its greatest glory under the Assyrian ruler Sennacherib (704-681 B.C.). An almost impregnable fortress, guarded by walls, moats, canals, the River Khusar, and outworks, Nineveh seemed indestructible, but there is some evidence that perhaps its downfall was brought about when it was flooded by the Babylonians (cf. Nah. 1:8; 2:6, 8).

The city was first unsuccessfully besieged by the Medes in 614 B.C., but when the Medes were joined by Scythian tribes and above all, by Babylonia, a two-and-one-half-month siege in 612 B.C. led to the breaching of Nineveh's wall and its downfall, marking for all practical purposes the end of the Assyrian Empire.

The Theological Context

On first reading, Nahum's prophecies seem to be nothing but nationalistic and vengeful celebrations of the end of Assyrian power. Such has been the judgment of most commentators and, indeed, of the church, which has never included readings from Nahum in its lectionary.

The truth is that Nahum is a magnificent presentation of the nature of God and should be preached as such. Its opening modified acrostic poem in 1:2-11 sets forth God's zeal for his purpose, his goodness, might, slowness to anger, and just retribution of evil. The oracles that follow are, literally, some of the most vivid war poetry ever written and portray God's absolute opposition to and victory over evil: 2:1-13 describes the siege and destruction of Nineveh by the scarlet-clad troops of Babylonia; 3:1-7 is a woe oracle over Nineveh, giving an example of her ruthless conquests, vv. 2-4, and then pronouncing judgment on her, vv. 5-7; 3:8-13 proclaims that as mighty Thebes fell, so shall Nineveh; and 3:14-19 contains a taunt song that tells Nineveh to prepare for siege, vv. 14-17. The chapter then ends with a funeral dirge over the fallen city, vv. 18-19. But there is nothing in the theology of Nahum that does not accord with the New Testament proclamation of the gospel.

NAHUM 1:2-11

Features to Note in the Text

The nature of God is systematically set forth in this opening poem, which some commentators want to call secondary, but which is absolutely essential as the context of the whole book.

God is a "jealous" God, v. 2. The word for "jealousy" can also be translated "zeal." God is a jealous, zealous God, working toward a goal and the fulfillment of his purpose. He will let nothing deter him from that purpose, which he is working out through his people Israel. Such is the meaning of "jealous" here.

God is "slow to anger," v. 3, but he cannot be mocked. He will bring his judgment on those guilty of evil.

God's slowness to anger is not occasioned by weakness. He is "of great might," as is illustrated in vv. 3c-5, in which the chaotic waters and all of nature are shown subject to his sovereignty over them.

God "will by no means clear the guilty," v. 3. So in v. 6, his judging wrath is poured out on the wicked, and none can withstand it.

But those who "take refuge" in God, v. 7, are known intimately by God, and they find him to be an unconquerable fortress in times of trouble and a shield from destruction in the day of judgment. Such is his goodness.

Part of his goodness, however, is also his defeat of all the wicked.

Vv. 9-10 are spoken directly to Nineveh, who will not have to be twice destroyed. God's judging wrath will eliminate Assyria, which has "plotted evil against the Lord" by plotting and doing evil against Israel, the instrument of God's purpose in the world.

Sermon Possibilities

1. God the Slow Avenger

If we read v. 1 in its Hebrew order, it has about it a drumbeat:

> A jealous God and an avenger is Yahweh,
>   an avenger is Yahweh and lord of wrath.
> An avenger is Yahweh against his enemies,
>   and a keeper of anger against his foes.

How are we to understand that?

First of all, according to Paul in Romans chapter 2, for example, we are to understand it in terms of a last judgment. There is a day of wrath when God's righteous judgment on all our sins will be revealed, says the apostle. "There will be tribulation and distress for every human being who does evil" (Rom. 2:9). There will come a time at the end when our Lord will ask us that final question, "What is this that you have done?" (Gen. 3:13). Why is it that you have not clothed the naked and fed the hungry and visited the imprisoned? Why is it that you have not sought me or known me, and have simply gone your own way? Why is it that you seek security in the things of this world and rely not on the Holy One of Israel? Answer me! Yes, there is a final judgment. In Nahum's words, "Yahweh will by no means clear the guilty."

But according to Nahum, and indeed to Paul, there is also a judgment now. Nineveh did actually fall in 612 B.C. because of all its ruthless evil. Nations still totter and disappear, and warfare still engulfs the earth. Tanks rumble, and missiles flash, and soldiers stumble over heaps of corpses (Nah. 3:3). Societies disintegrate, and families split, and we cannot get to sleep at night, for a jealous God, an avenging God, is the Lord of the church, who by no means clears the guilty.

Yet there is a word of grace in the midst of Nahum's terrible announcement of judgment. "Yahweh is slow to anger," writes the prophet. This avenging God is slow to anger — and how true that is to our experience of him! Think how long he put up with the follies and foibles and lack of faith of his people Israel! And then think how long he has put up with our equal shortcomings and sins! He has even been slow to threaten us. He has let us ignore the Book of Nahum for years. He has let us wander on our merry way and never shown us the disaster staring us in the face. He has let us play at being our own gods and goddesses, like children out-of-doors, engaged in charades, and he has been very hesitant to put an end to our game by telling us that night is coming. Slow to threaten, slow even to show displeasure has been this patient, long-suffering God of ours.

And then, when he has finally threatened us, how slow he has been to carry out the threat. "In the day that you try to be your own gods," he told us — "when you eat that forbidden fruit, when you try to go it on your own and make your Creator unnecessary — in that day you will surely die." But we have not yet died, have we, though the specter of death stands just outside the door. The nuclear missiles have not yet loosed their warheads, God's sun still shines on our land, and you and I still draw those breaths of life with which a gracious God fills our lungs. God is slow — very slow — to carry out his threat of death.

Yet, "Do you not know," asks Paul in Romans 2:4, "that God's kindness is meant to lead you to repentance?" God's call to us from Nahum is a call to repentance. I do not know your secret sins. Sometimes I do not even know my own. But I do know that we all have sinned and fallen short of the glory of God; that we are very concerned about ourselves and not about our neighbors; that most of our programs for reforming society are built out of our own conceit and not in reliance on God; that above all else, we want power for ourselves and not a humble dependence on the Lord; and that therefore a continual, trustful turning to him is not the way of our hearts. And in answer to that, the prophet Nahum tells us that God will by no means clear the guilty.

But God also offers us time — time right now to take advantage of the grace of repentance and forgiveness; time through the sacrifice of our Lord Jesus Christ on the cross. "The Lord is very slow to anger."

2. "Vengeance Is Mine"

The opening lines of this passage drum into the listener and reader the fact that God is an avenger against his adversaries. And many have thought that the oracles of Nahum are therefore evidences of Israel's nationalistic hatred of its foes. But that is a misreading of the text, and the repetition of the thought in v. 2 should warn against such an assessment of the prophet's work.

Israel is not the avenger in this book. God is. And Israel takes no vengeance against its foe. God does. Israel is but the passive recipient of the Lord's deed of salvation on its behalf, for the defeat of Nineveh means freedom and new life for Israel. Thus, the fall of Nineveh is called "good news," gospel, and "peace" in 1:15.

We worship a Lord who commanded us to forgive those who wrong us seventy times seven (Matt. 18:21-22), to love our enemies, and to pray for those who persecute us (Matt. 5:44). But that does not mean that there is no justice in the world which brings judgment on wrongdoers. Rather it means that we turn our vengeance, our hatreds, our complaints of injustice over to God. The apostle Paul puts it clearly:

Repay no one evil for evil, but take thought for what is noble in the sight of all. If possible, so far as it depends on you, live peaceably with all. Beloved, never avenge yourselves, but leave it to the wrath of God; for it is written, "Vengeance is mine, I will repay, says the Lord." No, "if your enemy is hungry, feed him; if he is thirsty, give him drink; for by so doing you will heap burning coals [i.e., of repentance] upon his head." Do not be overcome by evil, but overcome evil with good. (Rom. 12:17-21)

That is what Nahum knows: that vengeance upon ruthless Assyria will come from the hand of God and not from the actions of Israel. The faithful take their refuge in the Lord and find their stronghold in the shield of his power (Nah. 1:7). And they are content to let God work his retribution (cf. Jer. 11:20). That does not mean, of course, that we are not to work against injustice and evil in our world. But it does mean that we do not vengefully repay the evil person or nation for the wrong they have done.

Perhaps one of the best illustrations of that comes from the United States' treatment of Germany after the Second World War. There were those in this country who wanted to take vengeance on Germany by stripping her of her industry and turning her into an impoverished agricultural state. But those of a more Christian mind knew better, and the Marshall Plan was instituted to rebuild Germany into the democratic nation that it is today. Vengeance belongs to God. Forgiveness and love belong to those who trust the Lord.

Is it right to celebrate the destruction and fall of evil, then, as all the nations do at the end of Nahum's oracles (3:19)? There is a marvelous picture given in that verse of an uproarious sound rising up from the earth, because every people that has suffered under the Assyrian yoke is clapping in celebration of Assyria's fall. There was no less a celebration throughout the world when Nazi Germany fell to the Allies.

Yes, such celebration is legitimate, because finally it is a celebration of God's victory over evil. As the Psalmist sings,

If it had not been the Lord who was on our side,
    when men rose up against us,
then they would have swallowed us up alive,
    when their anger was kindled against us. (Ps. 124:2-3)

God works his justice in the world and destroys his enemies. The resurrection of Jesus Christ is the final evidence of that. And because of God's victory, all peoples can clap their hands.

NAHUM 2:13; 3:5

Features to Note in the Text

Both of these passages contain God's direct speech to Nineveh and begin with his announcement, "Behold, I am against you." Nahum 2:13 is the final verse of the oracle in 2:1-13, in which the Babylonian destruction of Assyria's capital is vividly described, and the reason for that destruction is given: God is against Nineveh, and so all of her instruments of war will be destroyed. She will no longer be able to assault other nations. Nahum 3:5 falls in the middle of the oracle in 3:1-7 and tells of God's shaming of Nineveh, pictured here in the metaphor of a harlot.

Sermon Possibility

1. The Determining Word

Paul asked in his epistle to the Romans, "If God is for us, who is against us?" (Rom. 8:31). His proclamation then was that no one can bring a charge of sinfulness that would lead to death against those who trust Christ, and nothing can separate Christians from the love of God in Christ, because Christians have been justified by the death and resurrection of their Lord.

But what if Paul's statement is turned upside down? What if God says to us as he said to Nineveh, "Behold, I am against you"? Is there any protection from death that we then might have?

Certainly God is the Lord over life and death (cf. Deut. 32:29; 1 Sam. 2:6). It is he who made us in the first place, knitting us together in our mothers' wombs (Job 10:11), breathing into our lungs the breath of life (Gen. 2:7), and sustaining us and all creatures alive by his gracious gift of that life, no matter what we have done (cf. Ps. 104:29-30). He alone can give us the gift of eternal life through Jesus Christ (John

11:25). But what, then, if the God who holds our lives in his hands is against us? Can we count on staying alive or inheriting eternal life? For that matter, can we count on any good — any forgiveness, any guidance, any sustenance of our life's goods and energies?

In line with Nahum's proclamation, can any nation or society count on its security and livelihood when God is against it? God is the sovereign who can "pluck up and break down," who can "destroy and overthrow" (Jer. 1:10). Thus, he can bring "princes to nought" and make "the rulers of the earth as nothing."

> Scarcely are they planted, scarcely sown,
>   scarcely has their stem taken root in the earth,
> when he blows upon them, and they wither,
>   and the tempest carries them off like stubble. (Isa. 40:23-24)

Assyria found that out when it defied God's justice for the nations (cf. Amos 1–2). And so glorious Nineveh fell, and with it the Assyrian Empire. Is not God's word in Nahum therefore a warning to us and to all peoples?

If God is against us, neither individuals nor nations have any hope of life or good.

Preaching from the Book of Habakkuk

Recommended Commentaries

Elizabeth Achtemeier. *Nahum — Malachi.* Interpretation: A Bible Commentary for Teaching and Preaching. Atlanta: John Knox Press, 1986.

Donald E. Gowan. *The Triumph of Faith in Habakkuk.* Atlanta: John Knox Press, 1976,

Charles L. Taylor, Jr. "The Book of Habakkuk. Introduction and Exegesis." *The Interpreter's Bible,* vol. 6. New York, Nashville: Abingdon Press, 1956.

The Historical Context

The book of Habakkuk is set against the background of the Babylonian domination of the Fertile Crescent, with Babylonia's defeat of Assyria and Egypt in 612-605 B.C. and its subjugation of Philistia and Judah in 603-597. Specifically, the book probably dates from the reign of the Judean king Jehoiakim II (609-598 B.C.).

In its opening chapter the book mirrors the injustice and violence of Jehoiakim's despotic rule (1:1-4), when forced labor, syncretism, idolatry, and persecution of the prophets characterized Judah's society (cf. Jer. 23:13-19).

Earlier in 622/21 B.C., good King Josiah (627-609 B.C.) of Judah had carried out a thorough political and religious reform of the nation's life. Asserting Judah's independence from a weakened Assyria and enlarging Judah's territory, Josiah ordered all foreign influences to be abolished, did away with alien cults and priests, centralized all worship at Jerusalem, and renewed the covenant between the people and God (2 Kings 22–23; 2 Chron. 34–35). Unfortunately, however, Josiah was killed in 609 B.C. at Megiddo, when he tried to halt the incursions of Egypt. Judah came under Egyptian domination, and Josiah's son Jehoahaz (Shallum) was deported to Egypt after only three months' reign. The Egyptian vassal Jehoiakim ascended to Judah's throne and totally reversed the reforms of Josiah. It is against this background that Habakkuk cries out, "O Lord, how long?" in the opening verse of his book.

The Theological Context

Habakkuk is made up of an extended dialogue between God and the prophet. Unlike most of the other prophetic books, it is not primarily addressed to the people, but rather consists of Habakkuk's prayers (1:1-4, 12-17; 3:1-16), God's replies to those prayers (1:5-12; 2:2-4); biographical (1:1) and autobiographical (2:1) material; resulting oracles directed to a general audience (2:5-20); and a psalm of thanksgiving (3:17-19).

Habakkuk's question to God is, How long will the Lord ignore Habakkuk's repeated prayers and allow evil to surround him on every side in Judean society (1:1-4)?

God replies (1:5-12) that such wrong is being punished by the invasion of the Babylonians into Judah. The Babylonians are worse than even the Judeans, however, and Habakkuk cannot understand why God allows an evil nation to act as his agent to punish evil (1:12-17). The prophet therefore takes his stand on a watchtower to see what God will say to him (2:1-4).

Habakkuk receives the reply of God: the Kingdom of God is coming (2:3). But before it comes, in the interim time, the righteous are simply required to be faithful (2:4).

2:5-20 is then an extended oracle concerning what will happen to those who are not faithful.

In 3:2-16 the prophet is further granted a vision of God's coming to defeat the wicked and to set up his kingdom on earth. And in 3:17-19, assured of God's coming victory over evil, Habakkuk utters his magnificent prayer of faith.

HABAKKUK 1:2-4; 2:1-4

These two passages are the stated Old Testament lesson in the three-year lectionary for Pentecost 31C. As such, they are paired with 2 Thessalonians 1:1-4, 11-12, which pictures the steadfast faith of the Thessalonian church, a faith consonant with that portrayed in Habakkuk 2:4. The gospel pairing is with Luke 19:1-10, the story of Zacchaeus, who is the opposite of the evil man portrayed in Habakkuk 2:9-10. The Psalm cited is Psalm 119:137-144, which is the prayer of one who does not neglect the Torah, in contrast to Habakkuk 1:4. Thus all of the paired lessons relate to one or another aspect of the Habakkuk texts, and they suggest three possible sermons from those texts.

Features to Note in the Texts

Habakkuk 1:1-4 is a standard lament beginning with the customary words of a lament, "How long, O Lord?" Usually laments are followed in the Old Testament by oracles of salvation, pronounced by the priests (see Isa. 43:1-4 for such an oracle). Here the lament is followed only by God's promise of judgment.

It is clear that the prophet has repeatedly prayed to God without effect. Habakkuk is a man of faith.

The key word in Habakkuk 1:1-4 is *mišpaṭ*, justice, which here refers not simply to judicial justice but to God's whole order for society's life. The Torah (v. 4) sets forth that order, and the meaning of Torah here is not simply "law." Rather Torah is God's teaching, the whole of Israel's traditions about what God has said, done, and commanded in Israel's life. Judah has forgotten all of that teaching, and so the Torah is "slacked." The order of God for human life is forgotten, *mišpaṭ* is distorted, and human evil reigns supreme. Moreover, human evil is so persistent and so widespread in Judah's society that it overwhelms the righteous, who are helpless to do anything about it.

The watchtower (2:1) here is symbolic, setting forth the prophet's persistent watching and waiting for some answer from God. The last line of 2:1 is usually emended to read "and what *he* will answer concerning my complaint."

The answer that God gives to his prophet is that "the vision" — that is, the vision of God's coming kingdom — is true. The time when

God again will set all things right on the earth, the time when his good order will be restored in society, is coming. God will restore the goodness to human life that he intended for it in the beginning.

But the coming of God's kingdom awaits "the time." That is, it awaits the time of God's purpose, not the time of human beings. In God's plan, the kingdom will be established at the appropriate time, according to God's timetable and not ours. Indeed, the Hebrew of 2:3 states that the kingdom "pants" or "puffs" toward its establishment. It "hastens to the end," and so the role of the faithful is to wait patiently for that coming.

In the meantime, however, before the kingdom comes, 2:4 sets forth how the righteous are to live. The Hebrew of 2:4 says that those who are "puffed up" will fail. That is, those who in their pride are trying to live their lives apart from God will not live. But the righteous will find life by being faithful. The last word in 2:4 is 'emûnâh, which has the same stem as the word "amen." It signifies steadfastness, relying constantly on God, putting one foot in front of another to walk in God's way, day by day, without ceasing. No matter what the situation, no matter to what extent one is surrounded by evil and violence, faithfulness is trusting God and continually clinging to his will.

"Righteouness" throughout the Scriptures refers to the fulfillment of the demands of a relationship. Those who are righteous in God's eyes are the ones who fulfill their relationship with God by loving him and trusting him and his commands (cf. Deut. 6:4-5; Mark 12:29-30 and parallels). Out of such trust there then flows a life of obedience to the Lord's will. In the Christian faith, it is Jesus Christ alone who perfectly loves and trusts God, and we are considered righteous in God's eyes if we inherit the benefits of Christ's righteousness by faith in him.

Sermon Possibilities

These two passages overflow with preaching possibilities. From the first passage, we could deal with the problem of unanswered prayer, or with the terrible weariness that we feel when we are confronted by society's seemingly overwhelming evil. The preacher might treat 2:1 and point out that finally all human means of establishing the good are inadequate and that in God alone lies our help and salvation. We could use the passages to talk about the persistence of faith in the midst of wrong and violence, using Habakkuk as the model and linking 2:1 with the text from 2 Thessalonians. A sermon could be preached on the necessity of establishing God's order in society. We could preach about God's sure promise of the kingdom "on earth as it is in heaven." Or we might deal with the meaning of "faithfulness" in 2:4 and what it means to "live." The possibilities are legion and those and many others have been dealt with in my Interpretation commentary. I will therefore mention only three others here.

1. What Is Faith?

We are told by a multitude of preachers to have faith, and Paul uses Habakkuk 1:4 to set forth the doctrine of justification by faith (Rom. 1:17). But what is faith? Does it consist in believing certain doctrines, or confessing that Jesus is the Christ, the Son of God (cf. John 20:31)? Does it mean trusting God in all circumstances or, practically, obeying his will? Certainly "faith" can include all of those things.

But here in Habakkuk, as in other parts of the Bible, to have faith means to believe God's promise and to act as if it is going to be fulfilled. For example, in Genesis 15:6, the aged Abraham believes God's promise that a son will be born to him and that he will have many descendants. And, says Genesis 15:6, it is "reckoned to him as righteousness."

So too here in Habakkuk, to have faith means to believe that God will indeed fulfill the "vision" and bring in his good kingdom on earth, and then *to act as if that is true.* It means to shape one's life according to the character of the coming kingdom — to be faithful and steadfast in obedience and love of God every day, because God is bringing to earth a realm of goodness and love and order. Faith means living in the light of that which God has promised and trusting that God will keep his promise.

For example, God in Christ has promised that we shall be with him in his kingdom and that he has gone to prepare a place for us (John 14:3). Well, what kind of person is fit to live with Jesus Christ? As 2 Peter puts its, since all of these things are coming to pass, "what sort of persons ought you to be in lives of holiness and godliness?" (2 Pet. 3:11). What sorts of persons should we be in light of the coming kingdom? Those who are humble before Christ's majesty, counting on his mercy alone? Those who have striven every day to love a neighbor? Those who have looked to Christ for every good and who have daily praised him for all his gifts? Those who have forgiven every wrong because Christ has forgiven them? Those who have not been anxious or who have not feared death, because they know their lives are in the hands of God? Those who have loved God with heart, soul, mind, and strength, in the power of the Spirit?

God in Christ has given us promises: "I am with you always, to the close of the age" (Matt. 28:20); "Whoever lives and believes in me shall never die" (John 11:26); "Whoever loses his life for my sake and the gospel's will save it" (Mark 8:35). God always keeps his promises. And faith means clinging to the promises, knowing that they are true, and living accordingly.

2. The River of Time

There is a temptation in our age, and in every age, to understand our lives in naturalistic terms, to fit ourselves into the seemingly endless cycle of nature's birth, life, and death. "A generation goes, and a generation comes, but the earth remains forever" (Eccl. 1:4). We raise our kids, and they raise theirs, and then those perpetuate the cycle — birth, life, suffering, death. It seems unending in its repetition. And after a while we have to ask, What is the meaning of it all? Is it, as Ecclesiastes says, "vanity," nothing but vanity (Eccl. 1:2), with no goal and no ultimate purpose for its continuance, a futile karma wheel of humanity's endless struggle?

Habakkuk and indeed all the Scriptures break that endless cycle of meaningless. Time is not going around in a circle. It is stretching out like a river. It had its beginning in the purpose of God, when he created our universe (cf. Gen. 2:4a). It flows toward the final fulfillment of his good purpose. God is time's Alpha and Omega (Rev. 1:8); he began it and he will end it. It flows from the high mountains of his will down all the centuries, until it reaches the great ocean of his kingdom, and the earth is filled with the knowledge of God as the waters cover the sea.

In short, time is linear. It had a beginning in God's act; it will have its end in the establishment of his eternal kingdom. Such is the message of Habakkuk 2:3. God is working toward a goal. He is working to restore his creation to the goodness that he intended for it in the beginning. And everything in the book of Habakkuk testifies to that working.

God controls the armies of the Babylonian Empire (1:5-11). He brings about the destruction of the arrogant and unjust and idolatrous (2:5-19). He is in control of all nature (3:5-6, 9-11). He brings his judgment on his enemies (3:12-15). Indeed, even the prayers and faith of the prophet are evidence of God's working in him. Time stretches out like a river in God's working toward his final victory.

You and I stand in that stream of time that flows according to God's sovereign purpose. Our lives are not meaningless repetitions, going nowhere at all. They are given us to contribute by faith and work to the flow of God's purpose. They are intended to carry us toward the goal of eternal life in God's kingdom.

To be sure, we can try to interrupt the flow. We can work against it, ignore it, believe it does not exist, struggle to dam up its effects in our world. We can decide that God is not at work and that there is no final goal to life. We can, in our supposed sophistication, sneer at the belief that there is a Kingdom of God coming, and decide that life is now as it ever will be, full of violence and evil and injustice.

But the prophet Habakkuk has written the vision large for us to read. And "the vision . . . hastens to the end . . . it will surely come, it will not delay" (2:3). That faith is held out to all of us who think that our lives have no goal or meaning.

3. The Puffed Up

If we translate the Hebrew of 2:4 literally, it reads: "Behold, the one who is puffed up; his life is not upright in him, / but the righteous by his faithfulness shall live." Those who are "puffed up" are contrasted here with those who are righteous and who live in faithfulness.

To be "puffed up" means to be proud, to rely on oneself rather than on God, to consider that all that one has and does is the result of one's own abilities and efforts rather than being the gifts of God.

For example, we enjoy a comfortable lifestyle. We have food and shelter and clothing, and we consider that they are all the result of our hard work. We have skills and abilities, and we think we alone have discovered and cultivated them. We have knowledge and technology greater than that of any previous age, and we congratulate ourselves on our superiority over the generations who have gone before us. We are a great nation, a mighty nation, stronger than any other on earth. Our scientists now can manipulate life and decide who shall live and who shall die. Our military can humble any foe who would defy our missiles.

Our wealth can work wonders in the world and prosper whole regions and peoples. And so we are tempted to strut through the earth and to declare, "We can do it!"

Indeed, we are sure that we know right and wrong, that we can be "like God, knowing good and evil" (Gen. 3:5). We have made "a name for ourselves" (Gen. 11:4) and are the masters of our destiny. We have found the way to wisdom (Job 28:20-23), and need not ever fear God to find it (Job 28:28). We are self-made, self-directed, self-fulfilling. We are the "puffed up," who think God is unnecessary.

Thus our lives are bent, crooked, distorted, "not upright," Habakkuk tells us in 2:4, not at all straight and in line with what they were created to be. God is the Creator, Redeemer, and Sustainer of our lives, and for all our pride, he alone determines our living. God alone, who is Lord over all, determines if our hearts are restless or if we have a peace passing understanding in him. God alone decides if we have gladness or if "all joy has reached its eventide" (Isa. 24:11). He alone can hear our prayers and forgive our sins and fill our souls with grateful purpose. God alone, say Habakkuk and all the saints, can give us abundant life to eternity, or he can let us inherit the death that we have fashioned for ourselves. Those who are "puffed up" will not live, but the righteous will live by their faithfulness.

HABAKKUK 3:17-19

Features to Note in the Text

This is the prophet's final affirmation of faith. Nothing has changed in his surroundings. He is still beset by evil and violence on every side. The Babylonians still overrun his country and mercilessly destroy and slay. The unjust are still abroad in the land, ignoring God's will and rule. But Habakkuk has been given the vision of the Kingdom of God on earth (ch. 3). He now knows who is in control of his life and of all life. And so he is able to proclaim that whatever happens, he can have joy in his Lord. God sets him in the "high places" — a sign of both protection and exaltation.

Sermon Possibility

1. Faith's Carelessness

This final confession of faith from the prophet reminds one of Paul:

> I have learned, in whatever state I am, to be content. I know how to be abased, and I know how to abound; in any and all circumstances I have learned the secret of facing plenty and hunger, abundance and want. I can do all things in him who strengthens me. (Phil. 4:11-13)

There is a certain carelessness about those of biblical faith. They find their strength, their sustenance, and their comfort solely in God, and so, in one sense, they can be totally unconcerned about what is happening around them.

That does not mean that the person of faith is not to be at work in the world, feeding the hungry, clothing the naked, welcoming the stranger, visiting the imprisoned, and working every day for the establishment of God's just and loving order in society. Our Lord commands us to do all those deeds, because they are finally deeds done to him (cf. Matt. 25:31-46).

But Christians know that the evil, injustice, and violence in the world are not the last word, just as Habakkuk knew it. Christians know that God is in charge, that his is the victory over all evil, and that his kingdom is surely coming, when death and crying and pain are no more (Rev. 21:4), and every tongue confesses that Jesus Christ is Lord (Phil. 2:11).

Therefore Christians are never crushed or in despair. They, like Habakkuk, know "that the transcendent power belongs to God" (2 Cor. 4:7) and that God will never forsake them. So they are carefree, relieved of anxiety about what will happen to them or about what the world is coming to. We know what the world is coming to. It is coming to Christ, and in that good news rest all our joy and hope and strength for living in this "meantime," before the kingdom comes.

Preaching from the Book of Zephaniah

Recommended Commentaries

Elizabeth Achtemeier. *Nahum — Malachi.* Interpretation: A Bible Commentary for Teaching and Preaching. Atlanta: John Knox Press, 1986.

Charles L. Taylor, Jr. "The Book of Zephaniah. Introduction and Exegesis." *The Interpreter's Bible,* vol 6. New York, Nashville: Abingdon Press, 1956, pp. 1002-34.

John Calvin. *Commentaries on the Twelve Minor Prophets,* vol. 4. Translated by J. Owen. Edinburgh: Printed for the Calvin Translation Society, 1948.

The Historical Context

Zephaniah's ministry took place during the reign of Josiah in Judah (640-609 B.C.). The materials in chapters 1 and 2 of the book were probably preached by the prophet shortly after 640 B.C. They reflect the syncretistic reigns of Manasseh (687-642 B.C.) and Amon (642-640 B.C.), who preceded Josiah to the Judean throne and who were totally subservient to Assyria.

As 2 Kings 21:1-5 and 23:4-14 show, those two kings allowed widespread idolatry throughout their realm: the worship, even in the temple, of Mesopotamian astral bodies and of Canaanite deities; sacred prostitution; child sacrifice; worship of the Ammonite god Milcom; and the equation of Yahweh with such foreign deities. Zephaniah 1:8-9 attests that Assyrian attire became customary in the royal court, and pagan magic invaded everyday life.

In 621 B.C., King Josiah instigated a widespread religious reform, based on the book of Deuteronomy (2 Kings 22–23; 2 Chron. 34–35), eliminating foreign practices and cults from Judah and centering all worship in Jerusalem. However, Josiah was killed in a battle with the Egyptians at Megiddo in 609 B.C., and pagan idolatry continued in Judah. Chapter 3 in Zephaniah probably was added to his book about 612-609, signaling the failure of the Deuteronomic reform to change Judah's religious practices in any lasting way.

The Theological Context

Forming the background of Zephaniah's preaching in 1:2–3:8 is his announcement of the imminent coming of the Day of the Lord, of that time when God will pour out his destroying judgment on all of his enemies, including those among his own people. Because of Judah's idolatry and indifference toward God (cf. 1:12), and because of the pride of the foreign nations (2:5-15), the Lord "will utterly sweep away everything from the face of the earth" (1:2).

God has repeatedly tried to call his covenant people, Judah, back to himself (2:1-4), but Judah has been unmoved by his instruction of them through prophet, Torah, nature, and military defeat of their enemies (3:1-8). Therefore the end is coming upon them and upon all nations (1:18).

There will, however, be left a remnant of faithful in Judah, who will humbly depend on God in fulfillment of their covenant with him (3:9-13). With these faithful God will rejoice and dwell in their midst as their King (3:14-17).

ZEPHANIAH 1:10-13, 14-18

In some lectionaries, vv. 14-18, concerning the Day of the Lord, are paired with 1 Thessalonians 5:1-10 or 4:13-18, and with Matthew 25:14-15, 19-29 or Matthew 25:1-13, all of which deal with eschatology. The church has always associated the Day of the Lord with the second coming of

Christ, with the last judgment, and with the resurrection from the dead. In such association, the passage has been used for centuries in poetry, hymnody, and literary works, as well as in the Roman mass.

Features to Note in the Text

The biblical concept of the Day of the Lord had its beginning in the so-called Holy War in the time of the Judges and the early tribal federation of Israel. At that time, it was believed that Yahweh fought on behalf of Israel against their enemies with supernatural means. The prophets, beginning with Amos, turned the concept upside down, however, and announced that the Day of the Lord would be the time when God would bring his final judgment not only on Israel's enemies, but also on his faithless people in Israel (cf. Amos 5:19-20; Isa. 2:6-22; Ezek. 7:5-27; Joel 1:15; 2:11; Mal. 4:5).

The description of the Day took on traditional features, many of which Zephaniah employs: the Day was the day of Yahweh's wrathful judgment on his enemies; it was a day of darkness and gloom, when the heavenly bodies would lose their light; human fortifications and wealth would be useless to defend against it; it would open with the battle cry of God the Warrior and with a trumpet blast; Yahweh's enemies would be dismayed and rendered powerless, and all would be searched out and destroyed, although a faithful remnant might be saved.

In 1:10-11, the Day begins in the commercial quarter of Jerusalem, and Yahweh searches that city for one faithful person.

"Thickening upon their lees" in 1:12 is a description that comes from wine-making. If wine is left undisturbed on its sediment ("lees") for too long, it can become thickened and syrupy, and its taste is ruined.

Sermon Possibilities

1. Worshiping a Useless God

In 1:12 of our passage, the prophet quotes a proverb that has been circulating through Jerusalem: "The Lord will not do good, nor will he do ill." In other words, the people think that God does nothing at all.

Such an attitude is prevalent in our time and perhaps in every time. God does nothing. He is not at work in the world. We see no evidence of his activity. If good things happen to us, they are the result of luck or of our own hard work. If bad things come our way, either we brought them all on ourselves or we're just unfortunate.

In short, we are thoroughly secularized creatures for whom God is absent from the world. God has nothing to do with the natural world, we think; that all operates by natural law. And God has no hand in national or international affairs. Those are determined by the politicians, the military, the terrorists, the multinational corporations. As for our own lives, what we make of them and what our fortune and destiny are all depend on us and our genes and environment. Those are the determining factors in our lives, not God.

Yes, perhaps we do believe in some sort of deity. Ninety-seven percent of the American people say they believe in God. But we do not count on him for much, though we may pray for help sometimes when we get in a jam. On the whole, however, God does not act. He is just "there," an unknown quantity in the great somewhere. He is like those idols of Babylonia, whom that great empire of people worshiped, but who could not act or speak or shape events, and who had to be carried from place to place (cf. Isa. 46).

What a contrast such deities are to the God of the Bible, who has the whole world in his hand! He delivered a people out of slavery and made them into a nation. He guided them for forty years through the wilderness and fed them daily with manna. He took them into a land flowing with milk and honey and defended them from their enemies. He gave them a davidic king and promised them a Messiah. He raised up prophets and psalmists and taught them wisdom and law. And when that people would not recognize his sovereignty among them, he sent them into exile in Assyria and Babylonia, scattering them abroad through the ancient Near East.

Then, when the time was ripe for his greatest work, he incarnated himself in his Son, and taught and preached and healed and forgave his disobedient people. Finally, that Son died the death that we deserved for our faithlessness, but the Father raised his Son from the dead. And persons who believed in him found themselves forgiven, made new and obedient, and sent into the world to tell all peoples what God had done.

Still today that God in Christ is at work through his Holy Spirit. Because of his powerful, faithful working, the natural world is sustained in its orderly round (cf. Gen. 8:22); the sun shines on the evil and the good and rain falls on the just and on the unjust (Matt. 5:45). Because of God's care for his creation, not a sparrow falls to earth without his will (Matt. 10:29). And because of his care for us, we are sustained alive by his breath of life (cf. Gen. 2:7; Ps. 104:29). Every day he guides us and watches over us and leads us gently toward his kingdom. Every day he prevents us from falling into temptation and forgives us for our wrong. Every day he surrounds us with the loveliness of his creation and with the love of our friends and families. Every day he strengthens us for the work he has given us and encourages our spirits. And when our days are at their end, he does not forsake us, but takes us safely through the valley of the shadow of death into the eternal light and goodness of his kingdom.

A useless God, a worthless God? Not if we believe the Scriptures! Not if we see his working by the eyes of faith in all of the events and circumstances around us. Our God is not dead and useless. He is the living God, the God who raised Jesus Christ from the dead. We have but to trust him to enter into his unceasing life.

2. The Day of the Lord

We live in a culture that does not believe in the judging wrath of the Lord. Probably the reason for that is that we have lost any sense of responsibility. In his book, *Whatever Became of Sin?* (New York: Hawthorn Books, Inc., 1973), Dr. Karl Menninger pointed out that the primary loss in our society is the loss of a sense of responsibility — of responsibility to God. God is largely distant or absent from our lives, and so he requires nothing of us. As a result, sin has no meaning for us: we are victimized by our environment or our genetic makeup or the way we were brought up; we do not actually sin. The mistakes we make or the bad things we do are really someone else's fault. We are just victims, and we cannot be held responsible. So, the logic runs, it would be totally unfair for God to judge us, and indeed, God does not do so. God — if there is a God — is only compassionate and loving and helpful. God is never wrathful; God does not judge.

Zephaniah 1:14-18 gives the lie to such an understanding of God and our responsibility to him. God will bring his Day of Judgment upon all people "because they have sinned against the Lord" (1:17). Nor is such an announcement found only in Zephaniah or only in the Old Testament. Paul is quite sure that there will be a "day of wrath when

God's righteous judgment will be revealed" (Rom. 2:5), and his constant prayer for his churches is that they may be found blameless on the Day of the Lord through their trust and obedience to Christ (1 Cor. 1:8; 2 Cor. 1:14; Phil. 1:10).

Indeed, according to the Gospel of John, with its "realized eschatology," the Day of the Lord began to come with the appearance of Jesus Christ (John 3:19), and how we stand in the judgment depends on how we stand with Jesus Christ. In the Synoptic Gospels, the Day of the Lord has its evidence at Christ's crucifixion, when there is darkness over the whole land from the sixth hour until the ninth (Mark 15:33), reminding one of Amos's words, "Is not the day of the Lord darkness, and not light, and gloom with no brightness in it?" (Amos 5:20). As Paul writes, "We shall all stand before the judgment seat of God; for it is written, 'As I live, says the Lord, every knee shall bow to me, and every tongue shall give praise to God.' So each of us shall give account of himself to God" (Rom. 14:10-12).

We are responsible to our Maker and Lord, and his question to us is the same question he asked at the beginning: "What is this that you have done?" (Gen. 3:13). It will do us no good to try to deny our responsibility.

ZEPHANIAH 3:14-17

In the three-year lectionary, Zephaniah 3:14-20 is the stated lesson for Advent 3C. It is paired with Isaiah 12:2-6, which is a song of trust in the Holy One in the midst of the people; with Philippians 4:4-7, which is Paul's call to rejoice; and with Luke 3:7-15 from John the Baptist's preaching of the coming judgment and of repentance.

The RSV has incorrectly joined the first line of v. 18 to the end of v. 17. Verse 18 is unintelligible in the Hebrew, and vv. 18-20 probably form a later Deuteronomic addition to Zephaniah's book.

Features to Note in the Text

Verse 17d should probably be read, "he will hold his peace in his love." The RSV has emended the text on the basis of the Septuagint, but the reference is to the battle cry of God the Warrior (cf. 1:14, where the "mighty man" refers to Yahweh). God the Warrior no longer wars against his people in the Day of the Lord. Rather, the Lord has taken away his judgment against his people (v. 15a) and done away with their enemies (v. 15c). The original understanding of the Day of the Lord, in which God fights for a faithful Israel against their enemies, has been restored, by the grace of God.

Sermon Possibility

1. Carnival

We have a picture in these verses of the people of Israel holding carnival, singing, rejoicing, shouting aloud in celebration in the streets of Jerusalem.

The reasons for the celebration are clearly given. God has removed his judging wrath from Israel and destroyed their enemies. And most wondrous of all, God himself is in the midst of the people, celebrating with them (v. 17). Fewer more radical anthropomorphisms can be found — God the "mighty man," God the "warrior" exulting there on the streets of Jerusalem with the remnant of his covenant people — that faithful and humble people described in 3:9-13.

This is a text for the church's celebration of Advent, and surely, the birth of Jesus at Bethlehem is God's descent into our midst, God with us, Immanuel. So Christmas is the time of the church's joy and celebration. "Joy, joy, Jesus Christ is born today!"

Further, that God in Christ chooses to dwell with his church means that he has taken away his judgments against us. We deserved the destruction stored up on the Day of the Lord's wrath. But God has forgiven instead, through the cross and resurrection of his Son, and those who humbly put their trust in him find their lives always accompanied by his presence. "Where two or three are gathered in my name, there am I in the midst of them" (Matt. 18:20). The church's proper mood at Advent is therefore repentance and thanksgiving for God's mercy.

Yet Advent is also the season of anticipation, of eschatological expectation, of waiting for the return of Christ to establish his kingdom fully on earth. The church and the world still face that final judgment of which both Zephaniah and Paul have spoken. And Paul still prays that the church may be found blameless in the Day of the Lord (see above).

The church knows that only through its trust in Jesus Christ will it stand in the judgment. But this passage in Zephaniah also tells us that the final outcome of that trust is joy, joy, celebration, carnival, and eternal life with our Lord. The kingdom of heaven a carnival of joy! Come quickly, Lord, yea, quickly come!

Preaching from the Book of Haggai

Recommended Commentaries

Elizabeth Achtemeier. *Nahum — Malachi.* Interpretation: A Bible Commentary for Teaching and Preaching. Atlanta: John Knox Press, 1986.
Joyce Baldwin. *Haggai, Zechariah, Malachi.* London: The Tyndale Press, 1972.

The Historical Context

Haggai's ministry was carried on entirely during the year 520 B.C., and each section of his book is carefully dated. Using the equivalent dates in our calendar, 1:1-11 comes from August 29; 1:12-15a from September 21; 1:15b–2:9 from October 17; 2:10 and 2:20-23 both from December 18.

During the ministry of Haggai, Judah was nothing but a tiny subprovince in the Persian Empire, and her inhabitants were in desperate straits. The only territory left to them after their return from Babylonian exile was Jerusalem and its immediately surrounding territory. While there were a few wealthy persons in Judah, most of the people were poor. Drought and resulting crop failure had left them hungry, and inflation had eaten up their meager resources.

The Judeans were subject to the control of Samaria, but they were allowed to have their own governor, Zerubbabel, who was the grandson of the exiled davidic king Jehoiachin (2 Kings 24:15). And they had their own high priest, Joshua, the grandson of the exiled chief priest Seraiah (2 Kings 25:18).

In 538 B.C., Cyrus of Persia issued a decree allowing those Jews who had been in Babylonian exile to return to the land of Palestine and to rebuild the temple, under the leadership of Sheshbazzar, a prince of Judah. However, the work was interrupted by the opposition of Samaritans from the North (Ezra, chs. 1–4). When Darius I, Hystaspes, took the Persian throne in 521 B.C., he ordered the opposition to the temple building to cease and commanded that those who had opposed it pay for its reconstruction and its sacrificial offerings (Ezra 5:3–6:12). It is in the year after Darius's decree that Haggai preached, and his concern is to spur his countrymen to resume their work of reconstruction of the house of the Lord.

The Theological Context

The principal message of Haggai is summed up in 1:7-8. "Thus says the Lord of hosts: Consider how you have fared. Go up to the hills and bring wood and build the house, that I may take pleasure in it and that I may appear in my glory, says the Lord."

Unlike many of the earlier prophets who opposed the empty ritualism and hypocritical worship carried on in the Jerusalem temple (cf. Isa. 1:10-17; Jer. 7:1-5), Haggai proclaims that the house of worship must be restored, in order that God may once again dwell in the midst of his people. Some peasants had been left in Judah at the time of the Babylonian exile, and apparently they had continued to worship in the temple ruins (cf. Jer. 41:5). But for the most part, the Judeans were cut off from their God. The Lord had sent them into exile because of their sin against him, and while some of them followed the counsel of Jeremiah (Jer. 29:7) and continued to worship in Babylonia, for most the covenant relation was a thing of the past.

Haggai's message, like Second Isaiah's, was that God had not forgotten them. The Lord would return to his people if they would return to him. Thus Haggai urged the Judeans to rebuild the temple, not in order to *earn* the favor of the Lord — the Old Testament rarely sees salvation as dependent on good works. Rather, Haggai urged the people to rebuild the temple as the outward sign of their renewed inner devotion to God. God promised to be with them (1:13; 2:4). He awaited only the response of Judah's heart.

HAGGAI 1:1-11

Features to Note in the Text

The hardships of Judah that are detailed in this passage are technically known as "covenant curses." In the covenant document of Deuteronomy, there are listed in chapters 27–28 both curses and blessings — curses that will come upon those who forsake the covenant to pursue other gods, and blessings that will be given to those who love the Lord with all their heart and soul and might (Deut. 6:4). The conditions outlined in this passage find their precedent in Deuteronomy 28:22, 23-24, 38-40. Haggai is concerned with covenant-breaking and covenant-keeping.

V. 7. The words "consider how you have fared" literally read in the Hebrew, "Put to heart the paths you have walked." Throughout the Scriptures, faithfulness to God is a matter not of outward show but of the inner devotion of the heart that issues then in obedience (cf. Isa. 29:13; 31:33; Jer. 4:4; Ezek. 18:31; 37:26-27; Mark 7:21-23 and parallels; Matt. 6:1-8).

Sermon Possibilities

1. The Futility of Self-Interest

Pictured in this passage is a people who resemble much of American society. They are a busy people, but they concern themselves only with their own self-interest. "My house lies in ruins," God tells them through his prophet, "while you busy yourselves each with his own house." Their concentration and activity are directed toward taking care of themselves, "looking out for number one," we might say, making sure that they themselves survive.

To be sure, they are undergoing hardships, and it seems natural that they would scurry about to find some sort of security for themselves. A few apparently prosper and are able to build for themselves comfortable dwellings, with rich cedar paneling. But most of the Judeans have to scratch out a living, and that is the focus of all their interests and efforts. Thus, when it is suggested to them that they should be concerned about rebuilding the temple, their reply is "Later. This isn't the time to worry about that" (v. 2). In short, prosperous or poor, their relation with God occupies no place in their thought and deeds. This is a secular people, who have forgotten about their Lord and who are relying entirely on themselves.

The New Testament has a great deal to say about such reliance. Our Lord puts it very clearly: "Whoever would save his life will lose it" (Mark 8:35 and parallels). Those who rely on their own powers to secure their lives will find no security, and those who trust only in their own efforts will never find satisfaction. Human beings were created by God to live in trust and reliance on him, and apart from that relationship, human life is characterized by emptiness and cynicism and finally death.

Jesus told the parable about the rich man whose land brought forth plentifully and who thought that he could just build a bigger barn and take his ease and drink and be merry. "Fool!" God said to him. "This night your soul is required of you. . . . So is he who lays up treasure for himself, and is not rich toward God" (Luke 12:16-21). Self-interest, it seems, pays no dividends. Certainly it was paying none for the Judeans in our passage from Haggai. They were, in truth, trying to save their own lives and were losing them instead.

2. A Tit-for-Tat God?

On the face of it, this passage seems to suggest that if the Judeans honored God by working to rebuild the temple, then God would reward them with prosperity. A sort of tit-for-tat religion: if you are nice to me, I will be nice to you.

A lot of people have that belief. If they go to church, God will reward them for their piety. If they help the poor, God will give them abundance. If they follow all the religious rules, God will bless them for their obedience.

Actual life does not work out that way, of course. We know lots of stories, at least from the newspaper, of scoundrels who are prosperous and comfortable and never seem to have any trouble. Criminals write books about their escapades and end up making millions. Psalm 73 vividly portrays such people:

> They are not in trouble as other men are;
> they are not stricken like other men.
> Therefore pride is their necklace;
> violence covers them as a garment.

Their eyes swell out with fatness,
  their hearts overflow with follies.
They scoff and speak with malice,
  loftily they threaten oppression.
They set their mouths against the heavens,
  and their tongue struts through the earth.
Therefore the people turn and praise them;
  and find no fault in them. (vv. 4-10)

The truth is that this passage in Haggai has no relation to a tit-for-tat religion. Rather, it is setting forth three points. First, the deprivation of the people is intended to remind them of their covenant relation with God, and even prosperity can sometimes do that: "Bless the Lord, O my soul, and forget not all his benefits" (Ps. 103:2). A rich man too can realize that all he has are gifts of God, and that finally he stands in relation to One beyond himself to whom he is indebted, and without whom his heart is always restless.

Second, the deprivations of the Judeans in this passage are symbols of the fact that life is impoverished and withers and dies apart from relation with the Lord. God is the giver of all vitality and good, and apart from God, life is barren and devoid of worthwhile result.

Third and most important, God here, through his prophet, approaches his people. He yearns to return to them and to dwell in their midst as their God, in fulfillment of the covenant relationship. If the people will begin the work on the temple, that will be the outward sign of their inward renewed devotion, their longing to restore their communion with the Lord of their life. We are dealing in this passage, not with externals, but with the movement of the heart — with the yearning love of God's heart and his desire that his people yearn for him also with all their hearts.

Significantly, therefore, in vv. 12-15 that follow this passage, it is the Lord's Spirit that stirs up Zerubbabel and Joshua and the remnant of the people to get to work. God always takes the initiative. The Spirit of God works through the words of his prophet to revitalize and prompt the people to return to their God. God wills to save them, as he always wills to save us.

HAGGAI 2:1-9

Features to Note in the Text

Part of the content of this passage is referred to in Ezra 3:10-13, showing that there was a celebration at the time of the laying of the temple foundation, but mentioning also the sadness of the elderly at the pitiful dimensions of the new house of the Lord.

In v. 3, the sentence "Is it not in your sight as nothing?" reads literally in the Hebrew "much more than nothing?"

The preacher should note the three-fold repetition of "take courage" in v. 4. The basis of that courage is the fact that God says, "I am with you." God promises to be with his people in order to fulfill the covenant that he made with them at Mt. Sinai after delivering them out of Egyptian slavery.

"In a little while" in v. 6 refers to an indefinite eschatological time in the future, when God will cause all treasures of the nations to flow to Zion (cf. Isa. 45:14; 60:4-7, 13; 61:6; Rev. 21:24), symbolic of the fact that all nations will come to worship God (cf. Isa. 2:2-4; Zech. 8:20-23).

Sermon Possibilities

1. Tears for the Church

Most of the mainline denominations in the U.S.A. are losing members these days, and the influence of the church on society seems to have been lost. Certainly present-day religious bodies issue lots of pronouncements, sending letters to the President, urging Congress to take particular actions, writing amicus briefs for the courts, and carrying on lobbying in the nation's capital. But all such activities seem to have little effect on the course of our society, and the media seems to take notice of the church only when there is some scandal or sensational happening to report. To be sure, many politicians give lip service to religion at election time, and more conservative groups currently appear to have some clout with government. But on the whole, the old-time mainline denominations appear to have lost their prominent role in shaping the course of our nation.

Those who know what a mighty voice the church once was in

America mourn such loss. Like the elderly men and women in this passage from Haggai, many in the older generation of churchgoers feel that the church has lost its glory. The past power of the church, the vitality of its membership, the magnificence of its services seem now to have become "as nothing."

Yet God says to his church as he said to the remnant of Judah, "Take courage . . . take courage . . . take courage . . . Work, for I am with you." God promised that presence with us through Jesus Christ. "Where two or three are gathered in my name, there am I in the midst of them," he promised his disciples (Matt. 18:20). We present-day disciples should be aware of just what that means.

God is with us! Can we imagine the powers that are available to us through that holy presence? This God of Haggai, the God of the Bible, is the Lord who raised up the Rocky Mountains and flung the stars across a billion galaxies. He is the God who created a people for himself and who has overcome every evil human attempt to do away with that people. He is the Lord who plucks up kingdoms and brings them down, the one who commands empires and nations and moves all history toward the fulfillment of his purpose. This God in Jesus Christ is the Lord who kills and makes alive, who created every form of life in heaven and on earth and under the earth and who, when death defied his rule, broke the power of death forevermore. Such a God of power, of mercy, of purpose, of faithfulness, is the God who is with us! Do we not then have every reason for courage in the face of our disappointments and failures?

This God of Haggai and of the canon does not dwell on the past, however. He takes the past and does away with it and makes us totally new creatures in Jesus Christ. And he does so because he is on the move toward a goal. Our Lord is no static God, at rest in his heaven. Our Lord is on the move toward the establishment of his kingdom on earth, toward the time when there will be no more tears or pain or sorrow and the knowledge of God covers the earth as the waters cover the sea. Is that not our reason to work, then, in building up his church? God leads his church toward the time of his kingdom come on earth, and he bids us trust him and follow him along the way.

2. The Silver Thread

"I am with you. . . . I am with you" (Hag. 1:13; 2:4). That promise of the Lord of hosts punctuates the preaching of Haggai, but God speaks it not only in Haggai's time. The promise runs like a silver thread through the whole story of the Bible. It was that promise that assured even the scoundrel Jacob that God would keep him wherever he went (Gen. 28:15). It was that promise alone that accompanied the shepherd Moses as he returned to Egypt to face the pharaoh with the plea to let his people go (Exod. 3:12). It was that strengthening word that armed Joshua as he prepared to lead the Israelites into the promised land (Josh. 1:5). It was that assuring word that prepared a youthful Jeremiah to prophesy, though the whole of Judah would turn against him (Jer. 1:8; 15:20). Psalmists celebrated that comforting promise (Ps. 46:7, 11), exiles found new hope in it (Isa. 41:109; 43:2, 5), and Paul continued his preaching in Corinth because God spoke to him those words (Acts 18:10).

Is that not the one comfort in life and in death that makes it possible to live our Christian lives? Before his ascension, Jesus Christ made that promise to all of us who are his disciples: "Lo, I am with you always, to the close of the age" (Matt. 28:20). Christ is with us always, in good times and bad, in sickness and in sorrow, at the moment of our birth and at the gates of death, and he will never leave us or forsake us. That is the one assurance given to us as we follow him to Golgotha. That is the one certainty we have when we marry and raise our kids, when we pursue our callings and earn our bread. That is the sure promise that is with us still when our hair turns grey and our limbs feeble. But through all of the joys and agonies of this life, and the days of eternity to come, God's word, Christ's word, is enough: "I am with you."

Preaching from the Book of Zechariah

Recommended Commentaries

Elizabeth Achtemeier. *Nahum — Malachi.* Interpretation: A Bible Commentary for Teaching and Preaching. Atlanta: John Knox Press, 1986.

Joyce G. Baldwin. *Haggai, Zechariah, Malachi.* London: The Tyndale Press, 1972.

The Historical Context

Most scholars now agree that the Book of Zechariah is to be divided into three separate books: I Zechariah, chs. 1–8; II Zechariah, chs. 9–11; III Zechariah, chs. 12–14, and each of the three books has its own particular historical context.

First Zechariah, chs. 1–8, which form a carefully organized and organic whole, dates from 520-518 B.C. Its date overlaps the ministry of Haggai by three months, and the condition of the Israelite populace is the same as that found in Haggai. Judah is a tiny subprovince of the Persian Empire. She is a struggling country, beset by drought and famine, inflation and internal turmoil.

Second and III Zechariah then are made up of collections of miscellaneous oracles, some dated earlier than I Zechariah, most later. They have been added by an editor or editors to the original prophecies of Zechariah. These, along with the book of Malachi, bring the number of the Minor Prophets to twelve, and all three additions begin with the words "The word [or burden] of the Lord." Thus, all of these books are dealing with Jewish life in the Persian period.

The Theological Context

The principal message of I Zechariah is that God has roused himself to complete his task of bringing his kingdom on earth (2:13), and I Zechariah is designed to portray that activity. In a series of eight visions, granted to him in prophetic ecstasy, the prophet describes God's actions by which the Lord will complete his will for human beings. Interspersed among the visions are also a number of prophetic oracles, as well as a prophetic symbolic action.

Probably the best way to encompass the rich variety of material in I Zechariah is to divide it into three sections. After the initial oracle in 1:1-6, we find the following:

Section 1, 1:7–2:13, begins and ends with the glad news that God has reelected Jerusalem and that he is bringing in the new age of his kingdom.

Section 2, 3:1–6:15, tells who will have authority in the new age; it begins and ends with the call for obedience to God on the part of those authorities.

Section 3, chs. 7–8, is framed with questions concerning fasting and describes the nature of Israel's life in the new age.

A closing oracle in 8:20-23 then portrays the gathering of all nations to worship the Lord at Jerusalem.

First Zechariah is clearly concerned with the coming of God's kingdom on earth, and portrays that coming as assured and effortless. Second and III Zechariah are aware of the fact, however, that the kingdom will not come easily. There must be battles with the evil that pervades the world. God is portrayed in II Zechariah as the Divine Warrior, and the figure of the Messiah figures prominently in the book. But the people reject their Messiah and bring God's judgment upon themselves. Third Zechariah then pictures the battle won, the whole earth cleansed, and all nations made faithful to God in his kingdom come on earth.

The book of Zechariah is so full of possible sermon texts that I cannot possibly include discussions of them all in this work. Every vision told by Zechariah prompts a possible sermon in one's mind. The oracles are full of teaching about how we are to live in the light of the coming kingdom (cf. 7:1-14; 8:9-19), while 8:20-23 portrays the hope of all the earth. The New Testament, moreover, uses a number of quotations from II and III Zechariah and applies them to Christ, drawing us into this prophetic book in that manner. A full commentary study of these three postexilic works will therefore reward both preacher and congregation. I will deal here with only a few of the most pregnant texts.

ZECHARIAH 1:7-17

Features to Note in the Text

This first vision of Zechariah is given him on February 15, 519 B.C., and he tells us that he saw the vision "in the night," which is probably an indication of an ecstatic prophetic state. The prophet is allowed to see into God's heavenly court, where God talks with his angelic messengers. (For a similar court scene, see 1 Kings 22:19-22.)

The details about the colors of the horses are really not important for grasping the message of the vision, and they probably would only confuse a congregation.

Note that the prophet is not addressed directly by God, as is usually the case in other prophetic books. Rather, God's words are mediated to the prophet by angelic messengers.

"Seventy years" in v. 12 is the traditional length of time given for the Babylonian exile that was understood by the prophets as God's punishment for Israel's sin.

While the foreign nations who carried Israel into exile were understood as instruments of God's judgment on Israel, v. 15 nevertheless asserts that the foreigners, in their pride and abuse of power, have subjected Israel to cruelty and oppression far beyond God's intentions.

Sermon Possibility

1. "An Accursed Happiness"

This first vision lets the prophet hear the angelic messengers declare to God, after they have toured the earth, that "all the earth remains at rest"

(v. 11). That of course sounds like a happy state of affairs, but it is what John Calvin called in his commentary on this passage "an accursed happiness."

It is possible for us to believe that everything is fine in a relationship or a society or a nation when actually nothing is fine in the sight of God. A marriage may seem to be tranquil and good, when in reality peace has been achieved in the relationship at the expense of one partner being bullied into silence and resignation. A society may exhibit prosperity and order for most of its populace and yet harbor a slum or ghetto where persons who are desperately poor and children who are hungry have no just recourse. A nation under a dictatorial government can appear to be ordered and secure and yet have bought its peace at the expense of the freedom of its citizens. As Jeremiah said of Judah in his time, false leaders were preaching, "Peace, peace," when there was no peace with God (Jer. 6:14; 8:11). So it is too in this passage from Zechariah. All the earth is at rest under the yoke of the mighty Persian Empire, but God's people are suffering, and his temple and holy city lie in ruins.

Human beings always create some sort of communal structures for themselves, but because we are selfish and sinful, those structures are inevitably flawed. That which we think is good may not be good at all, because it totally ignores the will of God, having been established by human beings solely according to their own plans and desires. It may yield tranquility, prosperity, and comfort, and yet be totally at odds with God's plans and purposes.

God has spoken his will into human life, and all the relationships that we establish on this earth are to be measured by that speaking, which is finally to say that they are to be measured by God's speaking incarnated in Jesus Christ and mediated to us through the Scriptures. Over against that measure of Christ's love and goodness, all human programs and relationships are shown to be lacking and provisional, even those created by the church.

The good news of Zechariah, however, is that God rises up to set things right and to establish his rule on earth. That is the sure hope of the people of God.

This does not mean that we are not to work for peace and justice and a good society in our time. There is no book that more urgently calls for such efforts than does the Bible. But it does mean that we are to rely on the Spirit of Christ working in us to achieve those ends rather than on ourselves alone. And it does mean that even when we achieve some good, we cannot totally identify it with the will of God. Our reliance on God at work in us is always imperfect. But God's kingdom will come, and faithful work will not be in vain (cf. 1 Cor. 15:58).

ZECHARIAH 2:1-5

Features to Note in the Text

In this passage the man with the measuring line is measuring the outline of the broken-down walls of Jerusalem, in order that the Judeans may reconstruct them as they were before the Babylonian capture and destruction of Jerusalem in 587 B.C.

Sermon Possibility

1. The Dimensions of the Church

Biblical Jerusalem was located on Mt. Zion, and I have always been struck by the fact that in Christian hymnody, Zion is identified with the Christian church. We sing, "O Zion haste, thy mission high fulfilling," or "Wondrous things of thee are spoken, Zion city of our God." Thus it is very much in line with Christian tradition to apply this third vision of Zechariah's to the church. On that basis, a lot can be said.

First, we note from this passage that the church is to have dimensions far beyond our customary expectations. The man with the measuring line is planning to rebuild Jerusalem's walls exactly along the dimensions of the old Jerusalem. And how typical that is of our attempts to build up the church! We will keep it just as it always has been. We will invite into membership the same kind of people to whom we have always appealed. We will carry on the same programs that have always satisfied that limited membership. Indeed, we may find ourselves imposing very sinful dimensions upon the church — shutting out from it those of other races or social status or class, those whom we feel would not be comfortable in our fellowship anyway.

But our text from Zechariah bursts through all such limited dimensions. Jerusalem, Zion, the church is to be inhabited by so many souls that walls will not be able to encompass them — persons of every race and background, persons whom we usually ignore, and yes, persons who live not a mile from our church and who will come in if we seek them out. Our prejudices, our customs, our ways are not to limit the church of Jesus Christ. Bring into it the whole world for whom God gave his only Son (John 3:16)!

According to our text, Zion, the church, is also to have no defenses, no rationalizing or self-justifying strategies. We try so hard to make ourselves acceptable to the secular society around us — watering down our doctrine to make it palatable, changing our language and revising Scripture to avoid hurting sensitivities, ignoring parts of the biblical teaching if they seem offensive, giving performances just to entertain, shaping our preaching and programs to merely secular needs and interests. When this happens the church merges into the culture around it and is no longer identifiable as the church.

At the same time we seek power for ourselves, setting up lobbying offices in the halls of Congress and thinking that we can build up the church by massive spending, better parking facilities, and skillful use of the media. We would like to make the church important so that society pays it homage, forgetting that we worship a Lord who hung totally powerless on a cross.

It is the power of God in that cross that alone is the church's justification and importance, the power of God that is wiser than the foolishness of human beings and stronger than the sinful weakness of the world. God is the "fire" round about the church, says our text from Zechariah — the burning love that can make its way in the world if we but proclaim it, the marvelous mercy that needs no justification beyond the depth of its divine compassion. Let the church be the church, with the fiery love of its God surrounding and defending it, and all the world will be drawn to its light.

The church also has a glory within it, says our text, a glory that does not belong to it, but nevertheless a glory that is present in its midst. The glory has nothing to do with a beautiful sanctuary or with the magnificence of the church's liturgy, nothing to do with brilliantly robed clergy and the soaring music of choirs. The glory has nothing to do even with warm fellowship and creative programs. No. The glory of the church is the presence of the living God within it. "Where two or three are gathered in my name, there am I in the midst of them" (Matt. 18:20).

The glory of the church is the presence of Jesus Christ, its risen exalted Lord. There he is in all of his transfigured glory, victor over all our sins and the finality of our deaths, full of compassion for all our hurts, comforter of all our fears, guide of our steps, strengthener of our wills, purest love forever full, forever flowing free. The light of the knowledge of the glory of God shines from his face and in our hearts. Christ with us, God with us. That is the church's glory.

ZECHARIAH 4:1-6, 10b-14

The past generation of preachers probably used this text more than any other from Zechariah. Today the passage is largely ignored because of its difficult symbolism, but its central message is found in v. 6.

Features to Note in the Text

This is the fifth vision of Zechariah, in which he is given to see a golden lampstand and its accouterments. All of the features of the vision are important.

The lampstand is a cylindrical column tapering upward, with an oil bowl on top. Around the bowl are seven smaller bowls, each holding seven wicks that represent Israel, the people of God who are to be the light of the world. But they cannot shine by themselves. Rather they must be fueled by the Spirit of God, represented by the oil of olives. The two olive trees on each side of the lampstand have pipes giving oil directly into the bowls. They represent the high priest and the davidic king, through whom the Spirit is mediated to the people. Significantly, neither of these persons is named.

The vision is anticipatory, portraying the new people of God in the new age of the coming kingdom.

Sermon Possibility

1. Not by Ourselves

The task given to Israel in this vision is to be a light to the world, drawing all people to it in order to worship the God of Israel. That was Israel's task from the first, to be a kingdom of priests, mediating the knowledge of God to the rest of humanity (Exod. 19:6). When all the nations saw Israel's salvation through faith, they would be drawn to Israel's covenant fellowship (cf. Isa. 2:2-4; 60:1-3; Zech. 2:11; 8:20-23).

But that is also of course the task given to the church. Like Israel at Mt. Sinai in Exodus 19, the church is a "chosen race, a royal priesthood, a holy nation," called to "declare the wonderful deeds of him who called [it] out of darkness into his marvelous light" (1 Pet. 2:9). Jesus, in his teaching, made that calling very specific. "You are the light of the world," he said (Matt. 5:15). "Go therefore and make disciples of all nations, baptizing them in the name of the Father and of the Son and of the Holy Spirit, teaching them to observe all that I have commanded you" (Matt. 28:19-20).

This vision of the prophet makes it very clear, however, how the church can be enabled to fulfill its mission — only by the power of God's Spirit working in it (v. 6). The church cannot draw the world to the worship of Jesus Christ by its own might and power. Its own resources are inadequate for the task, no matter how strong the resolve and how plentiful the personnel and funding. The church will "make disciples of all nations" only by reliance on the Spirit.

But whence comes the Spirit? Once again the vision of Zechariah furnishes us the answer. The Spirit is mediated by those two figurative olive trees beside the lampstand. In short, the Spirit of God comes through the mediation of the high priest and davidic king, who have now been combined together in the one historical figure Jesus Christ. Christ is our high priest, proclaims the Epistle to the Hebrews (2:17; 4:14), and he is our davidic king, announce the Gospels. The Spirit of God now comes to us from Jesus Christ. Indeed, the Spirit of God is Christ returned to us, continuing his work on earth (John 14:15; 16:7-15; 20:22).

The church can fulfill its God-given task of being a light to the world and of drawing all people into its fellowship of disciples only as it relies on the Spirit of Christ to nourish and to empower its efforts. "'Not by might, nor by power, but by my Spirit,' says the Lord of hosts."

ZECHARIAH 6:9-15

Features to Note in the Text

According to this passage, Zechariah performs what is known as a prophetic symbolic action. Such actions are common in the prophetic writings (cf. Jer. 13:1-11; chs. 27–28; Ezek. ch. 4, et al.), and they are to be interpreted as the Word of God is interpreted: they begin an action of God within history that will run its course, shaping and influencing events, until it is fulfilled.

The high priest Joshua is only a symbol, in this passage, of the coming Branch or davidic Messiah, who will come from Israel and be exalted over the people as their ruler and priest-king. (Cf. the comment at 4:11-14.) He will build the eschatological, glorious temple of the Lord that is to come in the future (cf. Hag. 2:6-9). Joshua therefore removes the double crown from his head, and it is placed in the temple, which was completed in 515 B.C., as a reminder of the coming messianic kingdom. In v. 15, Zechariah then admonishes the people to live in obedience and faithfulness, waiting for the coming of their Messiah.

Sermon Possibility

1. The Once Empty Crown

The crown that was placed in the temple, according to this passage, was never permanently worn during Old Testament times. It remained empty, because it was the crown intended for Israel's Messiah. I have always been fascinated by the mental image of that crown, glittering in the light of the candelabra, hanging unused, gathering dust through all the centuries, while Israel awaited her redemption (cf. Luke 2:25).

Through all the years, the faithful in Israel looked for one who might claim the royal tiara, one who would be the fulfillment of God's ancient promise to David that there would never be lacking an heir to sit upon the davidic throne (2 Sam. 7). Israel looked for a righteous king, a king faithful to God, who by the Spirit of God given to him would rule in wisdom and understanding, counsel and might; who would bring justice to the poor and equity to the meek (Isa. 11:1-5); who would give security and peace to the land (Jer. 23:5-6); and who would be like "the shadow of a mighty rock within a weary land" (Isa. 32:1-2). Through all the centuries, the messianic crown was there in the temple, empty and waiting for its proper recipient.

In the fullness of time, at God's time, that empty crown was claimed, and it was placed on the head of a suffering Messiah, dying upon a cross. "Here is your king," even a Pontius Pilate had to proclaim (John 19:14), and he would not change the designation (John 19:19-22). Jesus Christ, dying but raised, has been proclaimed our Lord, our King over all the world, "that at the name of Jesus every knee should bow, in heaven and on earth and under the earth, and every tongue confess that Jesus Christ is Lord, to the glory of God the Father" (Phil. 2:10-11).

Thus today in many of our churches, there is a crown suspended from the ceiling over the chancel, or a crown pictured above the head of a stained-glass image of our Lord, or a crown embroidered on our paraments and ministerial robes. Jesus Christ is that long-awaited Messiah of whom Zechariah prophesied. He is our King, yours and mine.

ZECHARIAH 8:1-8

Features to Note in the Text

We have a series of five divine sayings in this passage, each introduced with the prophetic formula "Thus says the Lord" (vv. 2, 3, 4, 6, 7), and all predicting what life will be like in the coming Kingdom of God. God, in his jealous love for Israel, rises up to deliver his people from their enemies. He returns to Zion to dwell in the midst of his people, who are transformed to be faithful to the Lord. The city is repopulated and the covenant is restored (cf. the covenant formula in v. 8: "They shall be my people, and I will be their God").

Sermon Possibility

1. The Playground of the Kingdom

The Bible contains a multitude of pictures of what life will be like in God's coming kingdom. We have only to read Isaiah 35 or Hosea 2:16-20 or Zephaniah 3:14-19 or Psalm 47 or Revelation 21–22 to have a dozen different images impressed upon our minds. None is so unusual and startling, however, as that presented to us by Zechariah in vv. 4-5 of this passage. Here we find no ethereal vision of a heavenly Jerusalem, no universal worship of the Lord by all nations. Rather, the portrayal is earthy and simple.

What will the kingdom be like according to Zechariah? It will be like a public park. There will be benches where the old folks can bask in the sunshine in enjoyment. No disease will have brought them premature death, no feebleness of body or mind will have impaired their ability to stroll out to the park to chat with their friends. They will be able to enjoy their lives, in their fullness of years.

Moreover, there will be children playing safely in the streets of that park, running and shouting in their games, with no evil to threaten them and no perversions to corrupt their lives. The streets of the kingdom will be fit for children, just as the children will be fit for the streets. It is a wholesome picture, an enjoyable picture, with life at its abundant best for old and young. Certainly it is a portrayal that captures our most cherished dream for the future. When God dwells in the midst of his people, children can safely play and old folks can have enjoyment.

ZECHARIAH 9:9-10

This passage forms the background of what is often called Jesus' triumphal entry into Jerusalem (Mark 11:1-10 and parallels; John 12:12-16). As such, it is appropriate for the celebration of Palm Sunday, although it is not listed for that occasion in the three-year lectionary.

Features to Note in the Text

The king who "comes" to Jerusalem in this passage is the davidic messianic king, known elsewhere in Zechariah as the "Branch" (3:8; 6:12). Thus his coming is the fulfillment of those earlier promises in I Zechariah.

According to the Hebrew of this text, the king has three characteristics. He is "righteous," that is, he acts as a king is supposed to act. "Righteousness" in the Bible denotes the fulfillment of the demands of a relationship. He is "saved" or "delivered," being given victory over his enemies by God the Warrior (9:1-8, 11-17). Last, the messianic king is "humble." His humility is not shown by the fact that he rides on an ass, however; Genesis 49:11-12 promised that the Messiah would ride on that animal, and such is a mark of messiahship. Rather the Messiah is humble because he is totally dependent on God for his station and rule.

Therefore it is God who will eliminate the weapons of war, according to v. 10, and who will then give the Messiah a universal kingdom.

The portrayal of this righteous king is undoubtedly intended to contrast with that of the unfaithful shepherds or kings of the people in Zechariah 10:2-3 and 11:4-17.

Sermon Possibilities

1. Doing Right in Our Own Eyes

At the end of the book of Judges, there is a sardonic sentence that reads, "In those days, there was no king in Israel; everyone did what was right in his [or her] own eyes." That probably is a good description of our own society. We all have our own definitions of what is right and what is wrong. Individual opinions and desires direct our lives, and we feel that no one else has the right to impose his or her morality and rules for conduct upon us. We are autonomous, independent individuals, subject to no one else's will but our own.

The Messiah who comes to us according to Zechariah, however, is the king whose sovereignty extends over the whole earth, and it is that Messiah whom the Gospels identify with Jesus of Nazareth when he rides into Jerusalem on that spring morning. Jesus is the Christ, the

Son of David, the King, who comes in the name of the Lord (Matt. 20:9; Luke 19:38). We have a Ruler over our lives.

In short, the Christian faith is not to be equated with unbridled freedom, in which we are self-ruling individuals, free to do whatever we like. No. We have a King, a Master, a Lord, who has claimed us for his kingdom and who has given us commands as to how we are to conduct ourselves. And only as we submit our ways to the rule of Jesus Christ, observing what he has commanded us, can we truly welcome him on Palm Sunday morning. "These things I have spoken to you," Jesus told his disciples, "that my joy may be in you, and that your joy may be full" (John 15:11). Palm Sunday is a joyful celebration for those who will have a king.

2. The Paradoxical King

We are very quick to identify Jesus Christ with the Messiah, promised here in the preaching of II Zechariah. We know that he fulfills all of the messianic expectations of the Old Testament and that he alone deserves those messianic titles of "Wonderful Counselor, Mighty God, Everlasting Father, Prince of Peace" (Isa. 9:6). His is the government that has no end and that is wholly just and righteous. His is the rule that can finally bring peace on earth and good will to those with whom God is pleased. Clearly Jesus is the Messiah.

The Gospel writers know, however, just how paradoxical is the messiahship of Jesus. When they quote this passage from II Zechariah on the occasion of Jesus' entry into Jerusalem, they omit its fourth line, which reads, "righteous and saved is he," because the cross still awaits our Lord in the Gospels' stories. He has not yet fully exercised his righteousness by delivering his covenant people, and he has not yet been saved from death by his Father. The grave still confronts him, and he has yet to fight and win the battle over it. The well-known Palm Sunday hymn encapsules the thought:

> Ride on! ride on in majesty! In lowly pomp
> ride on to die!

Our Messiah is one who must suffer and die, and his cross is his exaltation as King. Only as the Roman centurion watches Jesus breathe his last can he confess, "Truly this man was the Son of God" (Mark

15:39). Only when Jesus has finished his sacrificial task (John 19:30) is he exalted and crowned as Lord of all (cf. John 19:19-22; Phil. 2:8-11).

That is the kind of Messiah we worship — one who dies on the cross. And he tells us that if we would be his disciples, we too must take up a cross and follow him (Mark 8:34 and parallels). We too must be willing to die to ourselves, to our own desires and purposes, in order that God may work his will in us, just as our Lord died in order that God might save the world through him. A suffering, paradoxical Messiah is the King of our lives, one giving himself up totally to the Father's will. Those who claim to be his followers are to have no lesser commitment.

Preaching from the Book of Malachi

Recommended Commentaries

Elizabeth Achtemeier. *Nahum — Malachi.* Interpretation: A Bible Commentary for Teaching and Preaching. Atlanta: John Knox Press, 1986.

Walter C. Kaiser. *Malachi: God's Unchanging Love.* Grand Rapids: Baker Book House, 1984.

The Historical Context

Malachi's ministry dates from about 460 B.C., during the Persian period of Israel's subjugation. Jerusalem and its immediate surroundings form a little subprovince of the Persian Empire. The temple has been rebuilt for some forty-five years but is a rather mean dwelling compared to its former glory (cf. Hag. 2:3). None of the wonderful messianic promises of former prophets have been fulfilled. Judah struggles for existence in the face of poverty, crop failure, inflation, and moral and religious indifference.

The Theological Context

We find in Malachi a series of questions and answers between the prophet and his contemporaries, all set in the context of the covenant relationship. It has often been thought that such a dialogue is the result

126

of a sort of Socratic questioning and reply on the streets of Jerusalem, interspersed occasionally by prophetic torah or teaching. It has further been thought that the name of the prophet, which means "my messenger," is taken from 3:1.

It is my view, however, that we have in Malachi a court case, conducted according to the law of Deuteronomy 17:8-13. When any case was too difficult for the local courts in the town gates, the case was brought to the priest at the temple in Jerusalem to be decided by him, speaking in the name of God. In this book, the prophet is playing that role of the priest, and the title "My Messenger" is taken from 2:7.

Initially in the court case, the Judeans bring charges against God: that he has not loved them (1:2) and that he is not just (2:17). But the tables are quickly turned, with God bringing his charges against Judah: they have despised his name (1:6), been indifferent toward his worship (1:6), been wrongly instructed by the priests (2:7-8), been faithless to the covenant (2:10), followed the gods of foreign wives and entered into divorce (2:13-16), wearied God with their evil (2:17), robbed God (3:8-9), and spoke against him (3:13-14).

The Day of the Lord comes, however, when God will suddenly appear in his temple and the wicked will be judged (3:1-5; 4:1-4). But the faithful will be saved (3:16-18), and God's judgment will serve as a cleansing of the sin of his people (3:3-4). Moreover, God in his mercy will send Elijah before the Day comes to turn the hearts of the people to faith (3:1; 4:5-6).

MALACHI 1:6-14

Features to Note in the Text

God's charge against the people in this court case is that they have despised his name (v. 6). That is, they have not honored God's name by bringing him unpolluted and acceptable sacrifices. Instead they have offered God sacrificial animals that are worth nothing to them (vv. 8, 13, 14), giving God gifts that they would not dare to give to a human governor. More, they approach their worship as a wearisome duty (v. 13), yet they think to win God's favor by such worship (v. 9).

The references to the fact that God's name is honored in all nations

(vv. 11, 14) are visions for the future of the esteem in which all peoples will hold the Lord in the Kingdom of God.

Sermon Possibility

1. Wearisome Worship

We pray every Sunday in the Lord's Prayer, "Hallowed be thy name." And that means that we are praying that God's name will be honored and esteemed throughout the world when his kingdom comes on earth, even as it is in heaven — the vision in vv. 11 and 14 of this passage.

One of the ways that we hallow and honor God's name, however, is by the attitudes and actions that we bring to our worship. We can dishonor God's name if we do not approach him in prayer and praise as "a great king" (v. 14), as one who is worth all of our devotion, as one who is to be honored and loved above all else.

If we come to worship only out of duty or of a desire to be seen; if we come to sleep through the sermon when God's Word is being proclaimed; if we do not join in the singing of his praises, and pray in sincerity and truth in the prayers; then we are saying that God is not worth our attention and devotion in worship. We sit in his house and yet ignore his presence. We let our minds wander from his words. We do not spiritually enter into the company of his gathered people or know ourselves united with them and him in the Lord's Supper. We remain bored or uninterested spectators, silently witnessing to the fact that for us God is not worth all the trouble.

In short, we try to make God less than he is — a great King over all the earth, glorious in his love and faithfulness, just in his judgments, all powerful in his creation and sustenance, gracious and forgiving and merciful in his daily care and guidance of us.

If we truly know the character of the God and Father of our Lord Jesus Christ, we know that such a God deserves our life, our love, our all, and that we can never give him the full glory due his name. But with all our being, we will honor him in our worship of him.

(Perhaps the preacher will also want to note that the failure of Judah to take worthy worship to God is laid at the feet of the priests in the following pericope, 2:1-9. Priests' duties are enumerated in that passage: they are to preserve all the religious traditions of Israel that are now contained in our Scriptures. They are to instruct the people in those traditions, as we clergy are to instruct our people in the Scriptures and creeds of the church. They are called to insist on worthy worship, and they are to mediate the commands of God to the people. Finally, they themselves are to walk with God, in daily communion with him. Certainly if we clergy fulfill such a calling, then perhaps worship will not seem so wearisome to our people.)

MALACHI 2:13-16

Features to Note in the Text

The people have complained that God does not accept their worship, and this passage gives another reason, besides that one cited in chapter 1. The men have divorced their Judean wives and married foreign women, the implication being that the men have also taken to the worship of the wives' foreign gods.

Marriage took place at an early age in Israel, before the age of twenty. But the men of Judah have discarded the wives of their youth and turned to other women.

Such action is "faithless" (v. 15), a breaking not only of the covenant of marriage (v. 14) but also of the covenant with God. For God hates divorce, says v. 16, and it is described as "violence."

The reference to "covering one's garment" is to the male's practice of spreading his cloak over the female as a sign of his choice of her (cf. Ruth 3:9; Ezek. 16:8).

Sermon Possibility

1. Marriage as Discipleship

In our time, when many of the members of any congregation are divorced and perhaps remarried, this seems like a difficult text to preach. Yet probably no passage is more important for the church's instruction about Christian marriage.

There is a very high view of the marital relation here, and it is consonant with the teaching on marriage found throughout the Scriptures. Marriage, according to v. 14, is a covenant between a woman and a man, and it is a pledge to which God is witness. Thus, his grace is present to sustain the relationship.

The wife here is described as the husband's "companion," and that description accords with Genesis 2:18, in which the woman is termed a mutual helper, and with Ephesians 5:21, in which male and female are "subject to one another" in mutual service out of love for Christ. There is no rule of the husband over the wife here. There certainly is no thought of the woman as a material object, to be bought and sold, as is sometimes erroneously said of the Old Testament's view of the marital relation. No. Marriage here is to be characterized by companionship, mutuality, and lifelong covenant faithfulness to one another.

Further, such a faithful marriage is said to give birth to "godly offspring" (v. 15), and once again that is the ideal throughout the Scriptures. Children in a faithful marriage are raised up in the "nurture and admonition" (KJV), "the discipline and instruction" (RSV) of the Lord (Eph. 6:4). Such is God's desire.

Divorce that severs the faithful marriage covenant is therefore described as "violence." Surely no better term can be found for the breakup of a home, for anyone who has been through a divorce knows that it does violence to the love, the dreams, the hopes of both married couples and children. Divorce wrecks human lives; it violently disrupts the well-being of all involved. And while there may be special instances in which it is justified, it is hated by God (v. 16), because God does not want anyone's life torn apart. He grieves over what we do to one another.

More, this passage from Malachi tells us that what we do in our marriages has a direct relation to our worship of God. God will not accept the worship of the Judeans, because they are faithless in their marriages. In other words, we can deny our relation to God in our bedrooms and living rooms and dining rooms as surely as we deny it in our failure to minister to the poor or in our failure to act justly. As Luther once pointed out, we are commanded to love our neighbors as ourselves, but our nearest and dearest neighbor is our mate, with whom we live. Faithfulness in marriage is part of what it means to be faithful in our discipleship. And God asks faithfulness in our marriage covenant as surely as he asks it in all our service and in our worship of him.

MALACHI 3:1-4; 4:4-6

Malachi 3:1-4 is the stated Old Testament text in the three-year lectionary for the second Sunday in Advent, Cycle C. As such, it is appropriately
paired with Luke 3:1-6, which recounts the preaching of John the Baptist, the precursor of our Lord, and with Philippians 1:3-11 in which
Paul prays that the church at Philippi may be found "pure and blameless" in the Day of the Lord.

Features to Note in the Texts

"The messenger of the covenant" in v. 1 is the Lord himself, who will
suddenly appear in his temple in Jerusalem to usher in his Day of the
Lord, when he will judge the unfaithful, exalt the faithful, and set up
his reign over all the earth. His coming will be preceded by a "messenger"
who will "prepare the way" before him. The messenger is not named
here, but we learn from 4:5 that he will be Elijah.

"In whom you delight" refers to the popular Israelite expectation
that they would be exalted over their enemies in the Day of the Lord.
In the context, it is therefore seen to be an ironic phrase.

The announced refining of the covenant people starts first with
the priests (3:2-4), because it is they who have led the people astray (see
above, 2:1-9). When the priests teach the people rightly, then the population will bring pleasing sacrifices to the Lord, in contrast to those
polluted offerings that they have been giving (see above, 1:6-14).

The precursor of the Lord will come preaching a message of judgment that will convince the people to have faith (4:5-6).

Sermon Possibility

1. The Loving Warning

Throughout the Scriptures we are told that there will come a Day when
the Lord will return to bring our evil history to an end and to set up
his rule over all the earth. We pray for that end and rule every time we
say the Lord's Prayer: "Thy kingdom come, thy will be done on earth
as it is in heaven."

That is a hopeful prayer, for it marks the fact that the wrong and violence that we see all around us are not the last word. No. The Lord himself will come again to set things right, to do away with the evil that so mars our lives, and to usher in a kingdom of peace and goodness and love. We long for such an outcome of our history.

Yet, despite our longing, we are also unsure that we want the kingdom to come soon. After all, we are a rather comfortable people. Despite the troubles and sufferings that we experience daily, life on the whole is pretty good. We manage to live through our various crises, and when tragedies do strike, our faith helps us deal with them.

Besides that, we hear from the Scriptures that the coming of the Lord will involve his judgment of our lives. The sheep will be separated from the goats, so to speak, and only those who have been faithful will enter into God's kingdom of good. We're not at all sure that we can pass that test — that we will be found "pure and blameless on the Day of Christ" as Paul puts it in Philippians. We all have our sins, don't we, some public, some very private, and so we have to ask the question that Malachi asks, "But who can endure the day of his coming, and who can stand when he appears?" Can my life, can your life stand the scrutiny of Jesus Christ?

For that matter, is it really true that God is going to bring an end to history and come to set up his kingdom on earth? Or is that just a biblical fantasy, dreamed up to reassure us in the midst of troubles? We're quite sure in this atomic age that human beings can bring the world to an end. But God? Is God going to do that?

The answer of the Scriptures is that the Lord has come. We are going to celebrate the anniversary of his birth at Bethlehem. And he himself told us that the Kingdom of God was beginning to come in him (Mark 1:15; Luke 11:20). But after his death and resurrection, he also told us that he will return to bring in his kingdom in its fullness. At that time, we will all stand before the judgment seat of Christ (2 Cor. 5:11), and surely our only prayer will be that one of which our Lord told us, "God, be merciful to me, a sinner!" (Luke 18:13). But by that prayer of faith, manifested in all our daily living, we will be justified, and we will be counted righteous before our Lord.

Is that time coming soon, the time of the end, of the Day of the Lord? "No one knows, not even the angels in heaven, nor the Son, but only the Father" (Mark 13:32). But the messenger to precede the Day has already appeared, Jesus taught. John the Baptist, preaching by the

Jordan and baptizing, Jesus said, was Elijah, the one whom Malachi said would be sent before the final coming of the Lord (Matt. 11:14).

So the Lord comes. The messenger sent before him has appeared, and we face the decision of how we will stand in his coming. It is a loving warning to us — loving because God wants us to have eternal life, and yet a warning because, as Malachi says, the Lord comes in both judgment and love.

MALACHI 3:7-12

Features to Note in the Text

The gracious invitation in v. 7, "Return to me, and I will return to you, says the Lord of hosts" is found also in Zechariah 1:3. The passage indicates that the Judeans can show they have returned to the Lord by bringing the full tithes and required sacrifices to the Lord.

Tithes of produce and animals were given to the temple Levites, who in turn gave the best portions to the Zadokite priests for sacrifices to the Lord (Num. 18:21-32). Offerings were the portions of the sacrifices that were set apart for the food of the priests and Levites (Exod. 29:27-28; Lev. 7:32-36; Num. 5:9). They might also be gifts given to the Lord on special occasions, such as in payment of a vow (Exod. 30:14; Num. 15:19-21; Deut. 12:6, 11, 17).

Sermon Possibilities

1. The Law of Tithing?

The Lord accuses the Judeans of robbing him by failing to bring one-tenth of their produce and animals as tithes to the temple and of failing to give the necessary offerings that support the temple personnel and that exhibit the Judeans' dedication to the Lord.

We must not turn the text into legalism to demand that the congregation tithe to the church. Faithful persons bring their offerings of money and time and talents to God, not because they are commanded to do so, but because they want to do so — because they love the Lord and because they want to give back to him in gratitude something of the overwhelming multitude of gifts he has given to them. We love God and one another because God has first loved us. We cannot help but give of ourselves when we realize that God has given of himself completely on the cross. The foundation of all Christian generosity is the generosity of God.

2. Robbing God

There is nothing that does not belong to God. After all, he created the world and all that is in it. He created it good, and there is no good that does not come from God. Thus we sing, "We give thee but thine own, whate'er the gift may be. All that we have is thine alone, a trust, O Lord, from thee." By stinginess, cheating, selfishness, we rob God of what belongs to him, as the Judeans are said to do in this passage.

There are many other implications in this passage, however. Apart from our church offerings and service, we can rob God in all sorts of ways, and we do so daily.

We can rob God theologically by describing him as less than he really is. We can deny that he so loved the world that he gave his only Son, maintaining that Jesus Christ was not the incarnate Son of God but simply an inspired prophet or moral example. We can deny that God's Son took on human flesh and was tempted in every respect as we are, yet without sinning. We can refuse to affirm that God raised Jesus Christ from the dead and thus overcame evil and death. Indeed, we can even rob God by despairing of his forgiveness and doubting his love. In this way, we rob God of all his works of love, recounted for us in the sacred story, and make him an ineffectual deity.

In similar fashion, we can rob God of his lordship by refusing to obey his commands. We can neglect the needs of our neighbors or refuse to offer them forgiveness. We can follow our own wills and desires and never follow Christ to the cross. We can try to be autonomous, self-fulfilling individuals and care nothing for God's guidance of us. We can think of our happiness, our comforts, our goals as all-important, and neglect God's goal and purposes for our living. Thus we can try to make God less than our Lord, an indifferent object of religion.

Surely, too, we can rob God of the praise and honor due to him for all that he has done for us, never raising our voices in thanksgiving for his gifts large and small, never exulting in the world of wonder with which he daily surrounds us, never realizing that his mercies are every morning new and that we are surrounded on every side with mercy as if with air.

But there is another theft we perpetrate in our time that needs attention by us preachers. We rob God of his children, whom he has created. The Scriptures are quite certain that every child formed in the womb is "knit . . . together with bones and sinews" (Job 10:11) by the hand of God. In short, every child in the womb is a creation of God and belongs to him. Yet by law and social custom we have decreed that it is permissible to abort those children. Thus, since *Roe vs. Wade* was decided by the Supreme Court in 1973, we have robbed God of almost 38 million of his children — children who will never sing "Jesus Loves Me," children who will never be able to come forth from the womb to fulfill God's purposes for their lives, children who instead will be discarded as medical waste. God is deprived of those whom he planned, and we are thieves in his sight.

3. Open Windows

The Lord tells the Judeans in this passage that if they will "bring the full tithes into the storehouse," he will open the windows of heaven for them and shower down "overflowing blessing" of food and goods.

That sounds like a tit-for-tat religion, and it is the belief that many persons hold. If we are nice to God, we think, he will be nice to us, as if his mercies depend on our good will toward him — as if we are the ones who have to make the first move. Go to church, believe the doctrines, bring your offerings, serve your neighbors, and God will bless you with material good.

That is far from the intention of this passage in Malachi. God has always provided for the Judeans in his prevenient grace. "I have loved you," God says in 1:2, and the whole history of Israel could be recounted in support of that statement — God's deliverance of Israel from Egypt, his guidance through the wilderness, his election and love for his people like the love of an incomparable Father, his provision for davidic rulers over them, his constant rescue of them from their enemies, and always, everywhere, his forgiveness and mercy, despite all their sin against him.

That is our story too, is it not? — our redemption out of our slavery to sin and death, guidance by our Lord through all the wildernesses of our lives, our election as the children of God, a davidic Savior's loving rule over us, and always, always the forgiveness. "While we were yet sinners Christ died for us." God has always made the first move.

So what God calls for from the Judeans in Malachi's time, and always from us, are love in response to his love, trust on the basis of all that he has done, obedience out of gratitude for his constant merciful and forgiving presence with us.

Surely thousands of faithful Christians before us can tell us that for such a life, the windows of heaven are always open, pouring out good beyond all that we can ask or think. Who can recount the goodness of the Lord? Every morning his mercies are new, sustaining us with his breath of life. On every side we are encountered by his common grace that he lavishes on all — the sun to rise on the evil and on the good, and his rain on the just and unjust. When we err, he gently corrects, and when we fall, he enables us to rise. When darkness surrounds us, his is the light that is never banished and the presence that never leaves us. In his company, we know joy and hope and peace that passes all understanding. By his promise he banishes our fears. By his Spirit, he enables us to do the good. And always he provides for all that we truly need, so that we can be content in whatever state we find ourselves, setting us in the company of his people and never leaving us desolate.

As the Psalmist prays,

Whom have I in heaven but thee?
  And there is nothing upon earth that I desire besides thee.
My flesh and my heart may fail,
  But God is the strength of my heart and my portion forever.
                                                          (Ps. 73:26)

Index of Scripture References

Printed in the United Kingdom
by Lightning Source UK Ltd.
107837UKS00001B/115